# Antoine-Louis Barye

## THE CORCORAN COLLECTION

*The exhibition and this catalogue are presented*

*in commemoration of the bicentennial of the French Revolution.*

# Antoine

## THE CORCORAN

# Louis Barye

# OLLECTION

Lilien F. Robinson and Edward J. Nygren

## THE CORCORAN GALLERY OF ART

Washington, DC 1988

# ANTOINE-LOUIS BARYE
The Corcoran Collection

**Sarah Campbell Blaffer Gallery**
University of Houston, Houston, Texas

**The Dixon Gallery and Gardens**
Memphis, Tennessee

**The Corcoran Gallery of Art**
Washington, D.C.

**The Sterling and Francine Clark Art Institute**
Williamstown, Massachusetts

This exhibition and catalogue were made possible by a grant from the National Endowment for the Arts.

Additional support for the catalogue was provided by the Kathrine Dulin Folger Publication Fund of the Corcoran Gallery of Art.

The technical examination of the bronzes was supported by a grant from the Getty Trust.

Published by The Corcoran Gallery of Art
17th Street & New York Avenue, N.W.
Washington, D.C. 20006

Library of Congress Cataloging-in-Publication Data
Corcoran Gallery of Art.
    Antoine-Louis Barye : the Corcoran collection.
    Bibliography: p.
    1. Barye, Antoine-Louis, 1796-1875—Catalogs. 2. Sculpture—
Washington, D.C.—Catalogs. 3. Corcoran Gallery of Art—Catalogs. I.
Barye, Antoine-Louis, 1796-1875. II. Robinson, Lilien F. III. Nygren,
Edward J. IV. Title.
NB553.B4A4   1988      730'.92'4      88-30425
ISBN 0-88675-028-8

Edited by Nancy Eickel
Designed by Hubert Leckie
Typeset by VIP Systems, Inc., Alexandria, Virginia
Printed by Garamond-Pridemark Press, Inc., Baltimore, Maryland
All photographs of works from the Corcoran's collection are by
Joel Breger.

# CONTENTS

# FOREWORD

Antoine-Louis Barye (1796–1875) is considered to be a Romantic sculptor whose naturalistic portrayal of animals gives them the spirit, action, and freedom of the wild. Barye's career at its height (1831–1875) coincided with a period of great change in French political, economic, and social life. The time also brought increasing appreciation for the arts on the part of the government and the burgeoning middle class. Within a dozen years of the mid-nineteenth century mark, more buildings were erected in France than in the previous 200 years, and sculpture was an integral aspect of their architectural identity. The Barye bronzes in the permanent collection of the Corcoran Gallery of Art represent a major holding of this important French sculptor's work.

William Wilson Corcoran, the founder of the Corcoran Gallery of Art (1869), was interested in and collected outstanding examples of contemporary European and American art. Corcoran himself encouraged the acquisitions committee to purchase 120 Barye bronzes.

The pieces were exhibited in a gallery reserved for Barye, where they were enjoyed by the public and studied by the Corcoran art students. The works proved popular as they provided an exciting contrast to the quiet of the Gallery's Neoclassical sculpture.

This exhibition and catalogue are the result of a close collaboration between Lilien F. Robinson, Professor of Art History, The George Washington University, and Edward J. Nygren, former Curator of Collections at the Corcoran and now Director of the Smith College Museum of Art. We owe them both a debt of gratitude. Five of the essays were contributed by graduate students who worked with Drs. Robinson and Nygren, and they are to be commended for the quality of their efforts. Such a successful collaboration between a university and an art museum is something of which we can all be proud.

I would like to take this opportunity to thank my colleagues at the other exhibiting museums who have been strong supporters of this presentation from its inception: Marti Mayo, Director, Sarah Campbell

Blaffer Gallery, University of Houston; John Buchanan, Director, Dixon Gallery and Gardens, Memphis; and David Brooke, Director, the Sterling and Francine Clark Art Institute, Williamstown, Massachusetts. The Corcoran is pleased to share this remarkable collection with other regions of the country.

At the Corcoran, several staff members deserve particular mention. William Bodine, Assistant Director for Curatorial Affairs, admirably supervised the logistics involved in organizing the exhibition and publishing the catalogue. Dare Hartwell, Conservator, capably oversaw the technical examination of the bronzes, carried out by independent conservator Meg Loew Craft. Cynthia Rom diligently cared for shipping and insurance arrangements, and Mary O'Neill provided invaluable clerical assistance.

Financial support is always critical to the realization of an exhibition and catalogue. Primary funding was provided by the National Endowment for the Arts, while support for the catalogue was derived from the Kathrine Dulin Folger Publication Fund at the Corcoran. The technical examination of the bronzes was made possible by funds from the Getty Trust.

Dr. Robinson has asked me to express her gratitude to staff members at the Baltimore Museum of Art, the Brooklyn Museum of Art, the Fogg Art Museum, the Metropolitan Museum of Art, the Museum of Fine Arts, Boston, and the Walters Art Gallery. She extends particular thanks to Dr. Jeanne L. Wasserman for sharing her knowledge and insights on the Barye bronzes at the Fogg.

Finally, in recognition of Barye's contribution to French culture and the Corcoran Gallery's longstanding recognition of Barye, the Corcoran dedicates this exhibition to the bicentennial of the French Revolution. Created in the spirit of a new world and its democratic principles, Barye's bronzes bear testimony to the greatness of the artist and his patrimony.

CHRISTINA ORR-CAHALL, *Director*
The Corcoran Gallery of Art

Barye    Statuaire

Alphonse Louis P. Trimolet after V. Cleminat, *Bust of Barye*. 1875. Etching. George A. Lucas Collection of The Maryland Institute, College of Art, on indefinite loan to The Baltimore Museum of Art.

# I

# Barye &

# THE FRENCH SCULPTURAL TRADITION

Lilien Filipovitch Robinson

Antoine-Louis Barye (1796–1875) played a significant role in the redirection of French sculpture. His impact was initially acknowledged during the 1830s by an emerging generation of Romantic artists who "were astonished and enraptured. They found there what they had vainly sought for in the works of their elders, the true perception of life, of truth, and of liberty. For centuries animals had not been seen, either in marble or bronze, which were not purely conventional and entirely lacking in fidelity to nature. . . ."[1] Although this level of response was neither unanimous nor sustained, Barye remained a formidable sculptural force throughout the century. His works had an indelible effect on successive generations of artists.

While it is not surprising that Barye's sculptures found broad imitation and support from a diverse constituency, his *oeuvre* escapes a single stylistic definition. He has most frequently been viewed as a Romantic artist. Théophile Gautier expressed this opinion, characterizing Barye as a leading independent who espoused anti-classical ideas.[2] Other critics expanded upon this assertion, noting that at a time when Classicism had become stagnant and sculpture worse than mediocre, "Barye boldly and simply took nature for his model and guide, and began in sculpture a reaction analogous to the reaction which Géricault began in painting."[3] Nevertheless, a recognizable component of Barye's style was Classicism, the official style of his youth. To a degree, there were manifestations of it throughout his career. Yet the crystallization of his style also paralleled the emergence of Realism in painting. Both his subjects and

mode of expression link him to this movement.

Barye's stylistic repertoire was extensive. His sources included sculptures of Archaic and Classical Greece, republican Rome, and the Ancient Near East, Renaissance bronzes, works by Michelangelo, Leonardo, and Rubens, Rococo statuettes, English animal painters, and numerous contemporary French artists. No single approach prevailed. "The master of Barye . . . was not Michael Angelo, or Leonardo, or Delacroix . . . but the spirit of the age."[4] In short, Barye was ultimately eclectic.[5]

## The Artistic Climate of Barye's Time

The period of Barye's artistic maturity, 1831–1875, coincided with dramatic and complex changes in all aspects of French life. As a result of the revolutions in 1830, 1848, and 1871, France witnessed three shifts of government. The Revolution of 1830 ushered in the July Monarchy of Louis-Philippe, the Citizen King (r. 1830–48). Although the promise of political and social reform was not realized, life styles were affected by industrialization and urbanization, and the concomitant growth of the middle class. Transformations in literary and artistic styles occurred at the same time that artistic productivity, critical and public involvement in the arts, and government patronage intensified. The State employed artists on an increasing number of public projects and significantly expanded commissions to individual artists.[6] Over 3,000 paintings and sculptures were commissioned and fifty million francs expended on the purchase of art from 1830 to 1848.[7]

The Revolution of 1848 brought the abdication of Louis-Philippe and the brief triumph of the Second Republic. Vanquished by a coup d'etat, the latter was succeeded by the Second Empire of Napoleon III. During his reign (1851–70), which paralleled Barye's own general acceptance and success as an artist, there was a dramatic rise in the number of exhibitors in the Salon. While 1,664 artists submitted work to the Salon in 1850, only 303 had done so in 1810.[8] By 1870, 5,434 were exhibitors.[9] The refurbishing of existing structures, the ambitious renovation of Paris, and the erection of new monuments throughout France substantially increased opportunities for artistic employment. By 1876, 51,500 paintings and 21,755 sculptures had been commissioned, and 102,330 paintings and 10,700 sculptures had been purchased by the government of the Second Empire and its successor, the Third Republic.[10]

Although the number of paintings purchased by the State exceeded that of sculptures, there was also a substantial rise in the latter after 1830.[11] By the time of the Second Empire, sculptors were responding to a significantly expanded range of demands. They were involved in the decoration of secular and religious buildings and in the erection of monuments to contemporary and historical figures. They were generously supported by successive regimes cognizant of the value of sculpture in promoting dynastic ambitions, national pride, and historical tradition.[12]

Even though the public's support of sculpture paralleled that of the State, the acceptance of sculpture was understandably slower than that of painting. In many ways it was far less accessible; familiarity with the process of its creation did not exist. By the second half of the century, however, an essentially middle-class public had become increasingly aware of sculpture. International exhibitions and acknowledgments of French sculptural achievements further expanded patronage.[13]

While the response of the critics, whose opinions appeared in an ever growing number of publications, was diverse, lines of opinion became distinct during the July Monarchy. Conservative critics looked to the classical past, urging sculptors to emulate antiquity in search of the ideal. Progressive critics welcomed the experimentations of the Romantic school. Their Second Empire and Third Republic counterparts further recognized the significance of new generations of avant-garde artists as they bemoaned the persistence of a traditional, classically inspired and (for them) sterile art.[14]

Many commentators focused on the issue of the importance of sculpture and the public response to it. Some noted a certain indifference, which they attributed to the imitative nature of contemporary sculpture and thus its inability to become "a noble elevated calling."[15] Accusing sculptors of failing to identify their mission, these critics claimed that they could discern no movement in the direction of expressiveness and originality.[16] Charles Baudelaire's review of the Salon of 1846 exemplifies this attitude. Drawing a comparison to painting, he noted that at best "sculpture is a complement; at the beginning and at the end, it is an isolated art."[17] Although he asserted that an appreciation of sculpture does not require the sophistication necessary for painting, Baudelaire nevertheless identified an inherent problem of sculpture: the spectator cannot be certain of the point of view the artist wishes his audience to have. Conversely, "painting has but one point of view; it is exclusive and absolute, and therefore the painter's expression is much more forceful."[18]

Critics such as Baudelaire and Pierre Malitourne called for imagination rather than imitation. They urged sculptors to aspire to produce works equivalent to those of the great sculptors of the past.[19] Moreover, they pointed to a contemporary emphasis on technical virtuosity, viewing it as an unfortunate reflection of public taste.

Other critics, however, judged their age unprecedented in both artistic accomplishment and appreciation. In 1862, Viollet-le-Duc concluded, "In France, perhaps no other government has shown a greater interest in the arts than that of the present. Within the space of a dozen years more buildings have been constructed than since the time of Louis XIV. Painting has been able to create one of the greatest chapters of its history; sculpture has become exalted; our museums have been further enriched. . . ."[20]

## Directions in Sculpture

Three major stylistic directions are apparent in French sculpture prior to 1870: Classicism, Romanticism, and Eclecticism.[21] Emerging earliest and dominating the first twenty-five years, Classicism remained an identifiable style throughout the century. It reached its height in Jean Antoine Houdon's portraits. Subsequent generations, especially those trained at the Ecole des Beaux-Arts, transformed it into a style dependent on ancient sources and Renaissance prototypes. Works by Auguste Clésinger, James Pradier, Henri Chapu, and Paul Dubois provide examples of this. These sculptors won the support of conservative critics, but others were less favorably impressed.[22] In a more extreme vein, Baudelaire wrote, "An excellent proof of the pitiable state of sculpture today is the fact that M. Pradier is its king. Admittedly this artist knows how to do flesh, and he has his particular refinements of the chisel; but he has neither the imagination necessary for great compositions, nor the 'graphic imagination.'"[23]

A second school of sculpture, identified in its own time as Romanticism, developed as part of the upheaval of the 1830s. While it did not produce an impact comparable to that which affected painting, sculptors such as David d'Angers, Auguste Préault, Henri de Triqueti, and Barye embraced its tenets. To them, Classicism frequently seemed inappropriate to the needs of their society. It did not meet the Romantic challenge of "being of its own time." Lofty idealism and restraint seemed inconsistent with the turbulence of a passionate modern age.[24]

Romantic sculptors did not limit themselves to subjects acceptable to conservative officials of the Academy and the Ecole. Instead, they explored nature, exotic lands, the past, and their own contemporary world. Frequently they focused upon dramatic, emotionally explosive situations. Some, including Barye, turned to animal subject matter, which was previously considered appropriate only for small-scale decorative objects or as a complement to primarily historical themes. Emerging in the 1830s, these sculptors were called "animaliers."[25] The roots of the animalier tradition were in Near Eastern and Roman sculptures as well as in small bronzes of the Renaissance and eighteenth-century France.

Animalier sculptors contributed not only to the expansion of subject matter but also to the popular acceptance of bronze, a material particularly suitable to the small scale of the sculptures.[26] Objects could easily be modeled in clay, plaster, and wax, and the textures and details necessary for convincing representation could be faithfully translated when the bronze casting was made. Moreover, casting in bronze permitted the execution of large editions of the same piece, which were then affordable to a broad middle-class audience. Subjects ranged from animal forms to historical and mythological themes and portrait statuettes.[27]

Since these bronzes were frequently utilized as decorative items in the home, the sculptors were sometimes considered craftsmen rather than artists. Other consequences of the metal's popularity included the escalating demand for the small bronzes, which brought increased production and lower quality. The number of foundries rose dramatically. Mechanical reduction aids and cheaper substitute materials were used. Less expensive sand casting frequently replaced lost-wax casting, resulting in a loss in detail. By the second half of the century an electrotype process had been introduced that required less metal and thus reduced cost. Quality, however, was further compromised.[28]

During the years of the Second Empire, previously radical Romantic artists, including the animalier sculptors, were accepted. Variations on the Classical style continued and were applauded by many, especially official representatives of the arts. Some sculptors embraced Eclecticism, notably Albert-Ernest Carrier-Belleuse, Charles Henri Joseph Cordier, and Jean-Baptiste Carpeaux. They worked in a variety of materials and made reference to many past styles, including those of the Renaissance, Baroque, Rococo, and Hellenistic periods. Nevertheless, traditionalism remained strongly entrenched.

## Education and Exhibition

Until the reforms of 1863, the main vehicle of artistic education, the Ecole des Beaux-Arts, was supervised by the State through the Academy, which controlled the competitions, selected the professors, and determined the curricula. The first task of an aspiring young sculptor was to be admitted into the Ecole. This could be accomplished through a favorable recommendation from an established artist. Study with the right teacher frequently determined entry into the Ecole and later success in competitions, such as the important Prix de Rome contest.[29] Among the teachers most sought after were Dominique Ingres, Jean-Antoine Gros, Louis Hersent, Pierre Guérin, and James Pradier.[30] Admission requirements included a general examination in drawing and a series of competitions, *i.e., concours de place.*

Study at the Ecole centered around a series of contests. Students were in constant competition and were subject to official evaluations that affected their careers.[31] The decisive test was the Prix de Rome competition, which commenced in May and terminated in October. Conducted in three arduous stages, the coveted award provided for five years of study in Rome and promise of subsequent success.[32] Prize winners not only were expected to follow a prescribed course of study while in Rome but were also required to complete annual assignments, which were submitted to the professors of the Academy for examination and written critiques.[33]

This pedagogical system remained intact until 1863, despite protests by artists and critics. Some contended that few could maintain their integrity under such rigorous control; others asserted that the program destroyed originality. Numerous writers pointed out that the most talented artists had not always been awarded the significant prizes.[34] The work of those who had met with success was characterized as "cold, insignificant and even decadent."[35]

Although there were notable exceptions, an artist's dependency on the State extended to exhibitions. Virtually the only opportunity for exhibition was the annual Salon, which, despite reforms, was controlled by the government through the Institute de France until 1864.[36] For sculptors, alternative opportunities for exhibition were almost nonexistent. They were further handicapped by the cost of fabrication as well as by the size of a work. Private dealers who accepted monumental paintings for their showrooms were unlikely to display large-scale bronze, marble, or plaster pieces.

The tastes and attitudes of the Salon jury were clearly important considerations for an artist wishing to succeed within the system. During the July Monarchy, when the jury consisted of only members of the Academy, many progressive artists were denied admission. Even though Salon reforms in the 1840s brought relief—a reconstituted jury included non-Academy members and even participating artists—judging from the lists of those admitted, jurors still preferred sculptures in the "grand style" that conformed to a traditional classical vocabulary.

Significant changes did occur during the Second Empire. Those selected to serve on juries increasingly were less conservative. More lenient toward formerly ignored and criticized painters such as Camille Corot, Jean-François Millet, and Théodore Rousseau, they were also receptive to sculptors whose work had been rejected in the past. Restrictions on subject matter and material were relaxed, and innovative sculptors such as Barye, Préault, François Rude, and others were recognized.[37]

## The Stylistic Development of Barye, 1809–1875

The period of Barye's training coincided with the end of the Napoleonic era and the reestablishment of the Bourbon monarchy. Although there are a number of nineteenth-century biographical accounts, information on Barye's training, life, and especially his ideas about art is limited. He received his initial training from his father, a silversmith, through whom Barye learned basic techniques as well as the exacting execution of precise, intricate metal designs. This early training played a crucial role in Barye's subsequent attitudes toward sculpture and the relationship of art and craft.

His artistic education continued in a similar vein when Barye was thirteen years old. From 1809 to 1813, he served as an apprentice to Fourier, a well-known metalworker. At Fourier's, Barye learned to work in a variety of metals and stones. He also acquired skills essential to the execution of the small bronzes that later formed the heart of his artistic *oeuvre*.[38]

In 1813, he was drafted into military service. Although no documentation of Barye's responses to the disastrous Napoleonic campaigns exists, his employment as a member of the topographical engineer's brigade permitted him to apply his technical skills in the making of relief maps.[39] By 1816, when the reactionary Bourbon monarchy had replaced the Napoleonic government, Barye resumed his education. Now, however, he turned from craft to art. The desire to become a "grand statuaire," which persisted throughout his career, was strengthened when he entered the studio of the sculptor and painter François Joseph Bosio. Of this period Barye recalled, "Tormented by desire to become a sculptor, I concentrated on drawing and modeling . . . but was without direction. . . ."[40] In Bosio's studio he received his first formal training in the fine arts. Even though it lasted only one year, the period was important, for it introduced him both to the techniques of painting and sculpture, and to Bosio's style of Classicism. While he eventually rejected Bosio's approach, Barye did acquire basic skills and values, and his later interest in historical genre subjects and the delicate detailing of his pieces suggest the continued influence of Bosio.

Barye enrolled in the studio of Jean-Antoine Gros in 1817. His selection of a painter as teacher may appear curious, yet association with a progressive artist was compatible with Barye's emerging stylistic and personal preferences. These two years of study with Gros were important to his development, for in the painter's studio Barye was immersed in current intellectual and artistic thought.[41] Additionally, he was profoundly influenced by Gros' paintings, which combined a fiery Romantic mood, impasto brushwork, and accurate representations of the contemporary scene.[42] Barye's mature works reflect a sculptural parallel of that synthesis.

Barye's exposure to the system of artistic competition coincided with the end of his tenure in Gros' studio and his admission to the Ecole. In 1819, he received an honorable mention in an Ecole-sponsored medal competition for his relief *Milo of Crotona Devoured by a Lion* (fig. 1). The following year Barye received a second place medal. Although the more coveted prizes were awarded to others, Barye remained undaunted. He continued to submit busts, and historical and biblical subjects to the competitions and the Salon.[43] Despite this effort, he received no additional recognition from 1820 until 1831. Even though Barye was decidedly more fortunate than many other progressive artists whose work was systematically rejected by conservative, classically oriented juries, his success was clearly limited.

Still, Barye had other alternatives. His early training qualified him for a position in the workshop of a well-known goldsmith, Jacques Henri Fauconnier. There, from 1824 until 1832, he further refined his already impressive metalworking skills. Beyond his primary task of executing decorative gold and silver pieces, he also designed and cast small bronze animal forms. In essence, Barye's genesis as an animalier occurred at Fauconnier's.[44]

Fig. 1. *Milo of Crotona Devoured by a Lion.* Walters Art Gallery, Baltimore

Concurrently, Barye continued his fine arts education. In part, the pattern he followed reflected that of other young artists: he visited the Louvre to copy a broad variety of works by the masters, and he sharpened his drawing skills by producing portraits of his family.[45] Following the lead of more adventurous artists, Barye frequented the studio of a former model known as Suisse, where at little cost he could work from the figure in an atmosphere of lively artistic exchange. His interests and ambition were also vividly illustrated by his frequent visits to the Jardin des Plantes, which soon became the center of his studies as the best place to view wild animals under varied conditions. Barye recorded his observations in a notebook. His studies ranged from rapid notations to measured drawings, and they served as the basis for a broad range of sculptural pieces and watercolors.[46] Additionally, he examined the collections of the Jardin's museums of natural history, zoology, and comparative anatomy. Lectures on animal life and anatomy kept him informed of zoological developments.[47]

In making life studies at the Jardin, Barye, among others, initiated a practice adopted by various artists. His superiority in the thoroughness of his study was readily acknowledged. For example, Eugène Delacroix, Barye's frequent companion at the Jardin, noted, "I wish I could put a twist in a tiger's tail like that man."[48] Barye also traversed the streets of Paris, driven by "an insatiable curiosity." He spent hours "grasping the picturesque humor of the dog and horse market. . . ."[49] He carefully observed the behavior of his own pets, perhaps hoping that the study of domesticated animals would offer clues to the reactions of those in the wild.[50] In addition to these records of attitudes, movements, and expressions, he made anatomical renderings of live species and precise measurements of dissected animals.

This inclination toward naturalism and his technical approach were reinforced by Barye's readings. For example, he was strongly influenced by an 1801 treatise on the sculptural methods of ancient artists. He adopted

their technique of evolving the form from its skeletal frame outward to the external layer of skin.[51] Simultaneously, he kept abreast of contemporary scientific studies on animals.[52] At a time when the Classical vocabulary dominated and Romanticism was in its infancy, Barye was anticipating the general scientific orientation of the second half of the century.

Another important feature of Barye's life during the 1820s was his place in a community of artists, writers, and intellectuals that at various times included Paul Chenavard, Théodore Géricault, Delacroix, Charles de Sainte-Beuve, Alexandre Dumas, and Victor Hugo.[53] Although Barye himself was somewhat reluctant to express ideas, he was an avid listener, alert to such contemporary issues as foreign and domestic policy, state control of the arts, scientific and technological advances, and new literary and artistic ideas.

It was during this early period that Barye received initial recognition. Exhibited in 1819, *Milo of Crotona Devoured by a Lion* (fig. 1) both reflects his Classical training and affords an explanation of Barye's success at the Salon. While his adherence to Classicism is evident in the treatment of the human form, Barye did not merely copy Greco-Roman prototypes. Rather, he selectively incorporated aspects of the earlier tradition while demonstrating his own observations of reality.[54] This is especially evident in his rendering of the avenging lion. To contemporary audiences, Barye's lion was decidedly more convincing than the "conventional curly-pated lions which were produced by orthodox artists under the belittling but well-dressed architectural term of 'lions d'ornament' . . . the cold, smooth, and insipid sculpture which was then accepted in high places. . . ."[55]

Fig. 2. *Tiger Devouring a Gavial.* Louvre. Photograph: Musées Nationaux.

The effect of the life studies Barye executed at Suisse's studio and at the Jardin des Plantes as well as the metalwork he produced for Fauconnier is apparent in such examples of his early style. They combined idealized human forms and convincingly real animals with an artisan's love of decorative detail and carefully crafted surfaces. Barye also carried over his training as an artisan by casting and finishing the pieces himself. For him, the processes of creation and production were emerging as of equal value, thus further distinguishing Barye from the typical sculptor. He was asserting his artistic independence.

Barye's work was accepted in the Salon of 1831, where he received wide recognition. Of the variety of freestanding sculptures and reliefs he submitted, special attention focused on the plaster piece for *Tiger Devouring a Gavial* (fig. 2). Barye was awarded a second place medal for this 40-inch work,[56] which provides an insight into both the positive response of the critics and public, and the negative reaction of the Academy and the artistic establishment. Heralded for its novelty of subject and skill of execution, the work was simultaneously considered an affront to legitimate sculpture. Adherents of this view rejected its emotionalism, preferring idealized subjects and controlled treatment. In turn,

> the public was charmed and fascinated by a half-life group representing a "Tiger devouring Crocodile" [*sic*]. With ears laid back and eyes gleaming savagely, the tiger grasps the reptile with his cruel talons, and bites furiously into the scaly body, while the crocodile, winding its tail around the tiger's neck, doubles upon itself in fear and agony, writhing and struggling vainly to escape. Such realism in sculpture of animals, such forcible and passionate rendering of life and movement, had never before been seen. Indeed, the tiger had not been considered worthy of the honour of sculpture, much less the crocodile, for academic zoology recognized only two animals, the lion and the horse, and both had degenerated into mere conventional forms. . . . This group had therefore all the attraction of novelty of subject as well as treatment, and the leading critics joined with the public in pronouncing it the strongest and most original work in the exhibition.[57]

Progressive critics, especially those supportive of the new school of Romanticism, looked to Barye with enthusiasm. Some conservative critics also lent Barye support. Writing in the *Journal des Débats*, Delécluze recorded such a response as he hailed Barye's originality, declaring that the tiger and crocodile "formed a group that was so real and so frightening that the moment one focuses on them one is distressed. They . . . are rendered with such force and poetry . . . that it is the strongest and best work of sculpture in the Exhibition."[58] Undoubtedly, the positive reception of this piece reinforced Barye's determination to pursue his singular approach.[59]

Barye's 1831 Salon entries were instrumental in revolutionizing sculpture. To contemporary audiences, his animal figures, independent of man, represented a dramatic departure from traditional subject matter. These

Fig. 3. François Rude, *The Neapolitan Fisherboy*. Marble. Louvre. Photograph: Musées Nationaux.

exacting, realistic presentations, devoid of sentimentalization or decorativeness, and the selection of the savagely intense moment of confrontation were completely new. The acceptance of Barye's works and the commendation of *Tiger Devouring a Gavial* represented a turning point in French sculpture comparable to that of another work shown in the same Salon, François Rude's *The Neapolitan Fisherboy* (fig. 3).[60]

Although the general tenor of the Academy members, the teachers at the Ecole, and the Salon jury was conservative,[61] the critics and the public assumed a less consistent stance. While some influential critics raged against innovations in painting and sculpture, a group of progressive critics called for an art more appropriate to their time and looked eagerly to avant-garde artists for solutions. Other critics fluctuated and shifted their support.[62]

Despite its frequently conservative inclinations, the public was capable of surprising receptiveness. Gustave Planche's summary of Barye's achievements may explain the sculptor's popular acceptance in 1831: "He has at the same time respected the rights of the imagination and of science . . . it is seldom we find exactness consistent with invention."[63] The public was drawn to

Fig. 4. *Lion Crushing a Serpent.* Louvre. Photograph: Musées Nationaux.

Barye's technical virtuosity and his comprehensive knowledge of animals, which was a product of a singular preparatory process. In the final preparatory drawing and the sculptural piece, he rendered every "significant and salient detail . . . with an energy, a freshness, a refinement which was impossible to surpass. . . ."[64] Yet in spite of the success of 1831, Barye's acceptance was not assured until 1850. He continued to exhibit at the Salon until 1837 and to receive private and state commissions.[65] Barye also explored the private market, selling his work to financially modest patrons.

Maintaining the habits of his youth, Barye further expanded his intellectual and artistic horizons. His study of scientific literature, travel descriptions, history, and contemporary events was reinforced by the broadening of his circle of acquaintances. On visits to the village of Barbizon, for example, he established a permanent association with a group of painters who had a major impact upon his artistic development.[66]

Barye's experience in 1831 was repeated two years later in the Salon of 1833, when he entered a variety of works, including sculptures of animals and historical figures, medallions, and watercolors. Typical of his work from this period, *Lion Crushing a Serpent* (fig. 4), which

drew special attention and was purchased by the State, represented a totally new sculptural approach to the subject. As Planche noted, Barye's lion bore no resemblance to the artificial, stilted lions that adorned so many Parisian buildings. He had abandoned those lions "bedecked with Louis XIV wigs that are far from recalling the monarch of the forest. . . . No one can mistake the author's meaning. The observer has before him what he might see in a menagerie."[67] Barye's lion was convincing. Here was a beast responding with the full force of its savagery to an enemy's attack. The artist had defined every ripple of tense musculature, the furrows of the muzzle, and the fierce, anticipatory movement of the jaws. Writers who preferred monumentality, however, found this type of articulation—excessive. Even Planche cautioned that such extreme realism might result in the diminution of artistic qualities.[68]

Similarly, while the veracity of Barye's forms elicited the public's applause, conservative sculptors and professors at the Ecole were critical. At first they were startled, even intrigued, by his obvious skill, but ultimately they rejected his realism and lack of conformity to academic tenets.[69] Nevertheless, Barye's success at this time culminated in his being designated Knight of the Legion of Honor.

For Barye, the Salon of 1834 was essentially a reiteration of the previous year. The jury accepted seven animal pieces by the artist, whose impact on contemporary sculpture was articulated by Alexandre Decamps in his review.

> Academic sculpture, like academic painting, drops a degree lower every year, and loses in each struggle it sustains in the Salon some of the ground it has held alone [for] thirty years. A young man [Barye] has brought principles so new and so simple into the field of Art that no sooner is he understood then rhetoric is deserted to follow him; it is because disgusted with the geometrical stiffness of Institute statuary he has appealed to Nature from the routine of the Professors; and the fresh and lively inspiration characterizing the works of M. Barye was too strong not to have great effect on the popular vision. . . .[70]

Barye submitted fewer works than before to the Salons of 1834 and 1835. He may have been occupied with other projects, such as a commission from the Duke of Orléans for a complex table decoration and an assignment from the State for a monumental eagle for the Arc de Triomphe.[71] Despite such recognition, Barye's reputation still was not secure. Aware of the favorable response of the public and many critics to Barye's sculpture, the Institute and other members of the official art world cautiously formulated an unspoken "policy of deprecating him and treating him as a mere *animalier*, a modeller of animals, beings belonging to a lower rank of creation."[72] They also stressed that the diminutive scale of many of his figures reflected their decorative quality. Such works were, in essence, "paperweights" rather than art.[73] In this manner, Barye was systematically relegated to the rank of artisan.

Moreover, by 1836, the character of the Salon jury differed significantly from that of 1833 and 1834. Composed of such conservative stalwarts as Ingres, Paul Delaroche, Horace Vernet, and Victor Schnetz, the jury refused works by Delacroix, Paul Huet, Rousseau, Préault, and Antoine Moine.[74] The jury of 1837 was similarly conservative. As members of the Academy and artists with vested interests and stylistic convictions, they were frequently "hostile to new ideas."[75] That jury accepted two of Barye's entries but refused the five hunting groups he had designed as table decorations for the Duke of Orléans. It has been suggested that the rejections were in part manifestations of the resentment felt over the support Barye had received not only from the Duke and the Duchess of Orléans but also from King Louis-Philippe. Such negativism was intensified when the king attempted to intervene with the jury to have the hunting groups accepted. Some were clearly disgruntled by the royal patronage of an animal sculptor and maker of "paperweights" and "stuffed leopards."[76]

Although he served on the exhibition jury in 1848, Barye did not exhibit at the Salon again until 1851. Absence from the Salon may well have affected his artistic focus and some of his activities. His visits to Barbizon were now regular events. Like his compatriots Rousseau, Charles Daubigny, and Millet, Barye produced watercolors and oil paintings, yet his attention was directed to wild, exotic animals, which he placed in landscapes reminiscent of the Barbizon region. These works also differed from his sculptures in their primary reliance on imagination.[77] Under the influence of the Barbizon artists, Barye expanded his horizons even further by turning to etching and lithography. Although little is known of his success with etching, Barye did execute lithographic illustrations of animals for *L'Artiste*.[78]

Once Barye stopped exhibiting at the Salon, he was forced to promote his own work. This may have led him to a new level of involvement in the production of sculpture. In 1839, Barye established his own workshop and foundry, thus bringing creation and production under his control. Direct participation in every phase of the process guaranteed the high quality he demanded. The workshop manufactured a multitude of small bronzes through the lost-wax process, which Barye was constantly perfecting. He also experimented with sand casting, a method by which more casts could be made at lower cost.[79] With Barye's help, a revival in the popularity of bronze sculpture, especially small-scale works, occurred. Judging from the high levels of activity and subsequent sales, Barye's workshop was a success. Unfortunately, his talents did not extend to management. In 1845, he entered into a partnership with Emile Martin, who assumed control of the business aspects of the operation. Through Martin's financial support and effective management, the enterprise prospered.[80] A turn in Barye's fortunes eventually led to his financial independence. By 1857, he had settled his obligations with Martin and had retrieved ownership of the models of his bronzes.[81]

The establishment of this foundry/workshop satisfied Barye's concern over control of reproduction and finishing. Later, when he was once again dependent on other foundries, Barye remained involved in production, frequently altering and refining models before he ordered new proofs.[82] He continued to supervise the casting of his sculptures, insisting on the use of the "Barye bronze," a combination of tin and copper, to achieve the desired coloration.[83]

There can be little doubt that Barye proved instrumental in setting an example for other sculptors. Indeed, this mergence of art and craft, which became increasingly evident in the last fifty years of the century, was compatible with the important role of industrialization in French life. A growing number of patrons scrutinized the Barye sales catalogues. And Barye responded by providing subjects in various sizes and price ranges for collectors of diverse tastes and circumstances.[84]

Sculptures produced after 1839 represented both a further stylistic refinement and an expansion of the scope of Barye's work. Focusing on humans and especially animals, they ranged from ambitious groupings to relatively simple single forms. The modest income Barye

Fig. 5. *Theseus Fighting the Centaur Biénor.*

realized from these multiple works designed for a bourgeois audience was augmented by government commissions for sculptures of monumental scale, such as *Seated Lion* for the Louvre and *Eagles* for the Pont d'Iena. At the same time, Barye executed some of his most ambitious decorative pieces. Often employing themes from antiquity and the Renaissance, he combined technical skill with aesthetic refinement and thus helped to establish a high standard for the decorative arts.

With the Revolution of 1848 and the short-lived Second Republic came major changes, particularly liberalization in government, economics, and education. These advances were paralleled by reforms in the arts. Barye was directly affected when the government, via its new Minister of the Interior, Ledru-Rollin, tried to make amends for the State's previous slighting of progressive artists. In 1848, Barye was appointed curator of casts at the Louvre and a member of the sculpture section of the

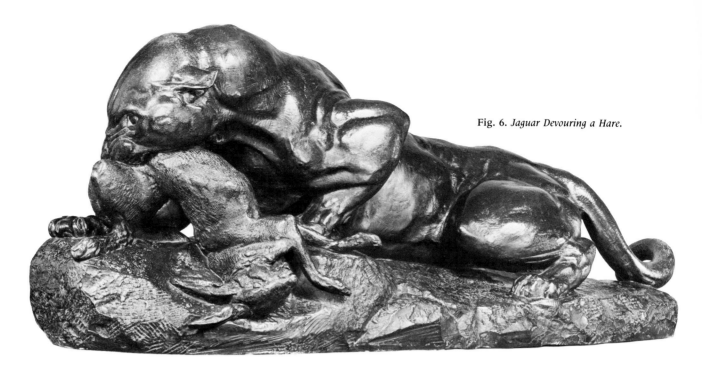

Salon jury. Although his position at the Louvre was terminated in 1850, he continued to serve on Salon juries.

The Salon of 1850–51 marked Barye's return to official exhibitions and a shift in his stylistic orientation. *Theseus Fighting the Centaur Biénor* (fig. 5) and *Jaguar Devouring a Hare* (fig. 6) were enthusiastically received by the public and critics alike. Both pieces not only retain Barye's typical juxtaposition of naturalistic details and emotionally charged moments, but they also reveal distinct changes from his earlier works, such as *Lion Crushing a Serpent.* Evident are a broader modeling, a generalization of details and surface, and in the case of the Theseus group, a different thematic emphasis. These features have been viewed as Barye's concession to a Classical style.[85] While Barye's studies of Roman marbles and bronzes, and his drawings after John Flaxman support that contention,[86] this was neither a new orientation nor the triumph of a single approach.[87] Greco-Roman art served as one of Barye's many sources throughout his career. His works of 1850 and later defy a single classification; rather, they represent a conscious adaptation of numerous sources.

Favorable responses to Barye's work in 1851 are exemplified by Gustave Planche's comments, in which he described the artist's entries as "the crowning glory of his experimentation of twenty years."[88] Planche identified the Theseus group as a major artistic challenge. He noted that although the subject had a widely acclaimed prototype in the Parthenon sculptures, Barye had succeeded in what seemed initially impossible, "deviating from antiquity without contradicting it . . . achieving a comparable level of idealism through his study of reality."[89]

Barye shared in the general prosperity and richness of artistic productivity of the Second Empire (1852–70) and received major government commissions. In 1853, he was given an assignment for four monumental

groupings of War, Peace, Order, and Force (fig. 7) for the Louvre's Cour du Carrousel, an appointment to the professorship of drawing at the Jardin des Plantes, and positive critical reviews. At the Universal Exposition of 1855, he was awarded the Grand Medal of Honor for his earlier Salon entry, *Jaguar Devouring a Hare* (fig. 6), which drew both laudatory and critically perceptive commentaries, such as that by Théophile Gautier. "Barye does not treat the animal form strictly from a zoological point of view. He agrandizes, he simplifies and idealizes and gives style to the forms. He has a fierce, energetic and rude manner which makes him the Michaelangelo of the menagerie."[90]

Even as his importance to French sculpture was being acknowledged, Barye continued his involvement in the decorative arts. At the 1855 Universal Exhibition, he exhibited his work in both the sculpture and the industrial arts sections. Some writers hailed this as evidence of Barye's dualism as sculptor and metalworker.[91] Implicit in such characterizations may have been the intimation of an artistic conflict. Conversely, it may be suggested that Barye, who never abandoned his initial training, was signaling not only an equality but also a synthesis of art and craft.

Participation in the Universal Exposition and subsequent Salons contributed to Barye's widespread recognition.[92] He received additional appointments and honors, including being made an Officer in the Legion of Honor in 1855 and elected into the membership of the Institute of Fine Arts in 1868. He was named to the selection committee for the London International Exposition in 1861. Two years later he was selected president of a consultative committee for the Central Union of Arts Applied to Industry. Amidst this activity, Barye sustained a high level of productivity from 1855 until his death in 1875. While he continued to fill requests for

Fig. 7. *Order*. Plaster. Louvre.
Photograph: Musées Nationaux.

his bronzes, he also executed large-scale sculptures. Commissions for two monuments to Napoleon I, mythological figures for the Louvre, and monumental animal figures designed for the Chateau d'Eau in Marseilles clearly indicate that he was being acknowledged as a "statuaire." Even though his obvious affinity with animal sculpture was consistently recognized, Barye's rendering of human form elicited commentary. Some questioned his skill.[93] Others praised him for his originality, a sentiment typically echoed in later assessments.

His human statuary is unlike that of the century . . . as if it had been evoked out of sources quite different from those drained by other sculptors. . . . His statues of men . . . are unmistakably genuine, unmistakably Barye, the work of a

11

Fig. 8. Jean-Baptiste (called Auguste) Clésinger, *Woman Bitten by a Snake*. Marble. Musée d'Orsay. Photograph: Musées Nationaux.

master more truly representative of France than any native since Goujon and Puget.[94]

A comparison of Barye's figures, such as his 1850 *Theseus Fighting the Centaur Biénor* (fig. 5), with popular contemporary sculptures, such as Clésinger's *Woman Bitten by a Snake* (fig. 8) from the Salon of 1847, is revealing. Although Barye's references to antiquity are apparent and the figures appear to parallel the idealized forms of the day, there are underlying differences. Distinguishing Barye's work are the scientific preparation evident in the realistic detail of the figures as well as their expression of passions. Even when Barye employed a classical vocabulary, figures such as those of the Cour du Carrousel (fig. 7) project a spirited strength and simple emotion to which the viewer easily relates. Clearly, Barye was equally at ease with human and animal forms, and he received commissions for both until his death.

## Barye and the Animalier Tradition

Despite consistent demonstrations of his artistic versatility and breadth, Barye was persistently viewed as an animalier. His sympathizers and Barye himself were cognizant of the underlying prejudice towards animal sculptures, both in regard to subject and scale.[95]

To some extent Barye overcame these prejudices. Even though the small pieces served a decorative function in the homes of his patrons, they were nonetheless acknowledged as works of art.[96] While he bridged the chasm between art and craft, "Even Barye could not entirely live down the old sneer against the animalist, a sneer which became popular and acute during his later years, owing to the aggravated polemic between religionists and evolutionists."[97]

Many critics and artists concluded, however, that Barye was "one of the most important artists of all time

Fig. 9. Christophe Fratin, *Lion and Snake*. Bronze. The Baltimore Museum of Art, Gift of C. Morgan Marshall.

Fig. 10. Pierre-Jules Mêne, *After the Hunt in Scotland*. Bronze. Photograph courtesy of Christie, Manson and Woods, Ltd.

. . . best compared to Balzac. Barye has an understanding of animal instinct and renders the form with a power equal to the effort Balzac placed in his passionate examination of the human heart which he so forcefully interpreted. Both have left an indelible impact."[98]

Barye's role in the rise of animalier sculpture is undisputed, yet he did not initiate this form. As early as 1831 and until 1862, Christophe Fratin exhibited sculptures of both domestic and wild animals (fig. 9), and his renderings of horses proved popular on the continent and in England. Another early exhibitor, Joseph Raymond Gayrard, participated in the Salon with regularity and success beginning in 1831. Both sculptors had little difficulty in gaining acceptance, although neither produced the complex, animated groups associated with Barye. Indeed, both preferred tamer, controlled forms, particularly in Gayrard's case, where human figures were frequently incorporated into groups of animals. Other animaliers of the 1830s and 1840s whose works were accepted into the Salon included Jean François

Théodore Gechter, Hippolyte Heizler, Henri-Alfred-Marie Jacquemart, Pierre Louis Rouillard, and Pierre-Jules Mêne.[99] Of this group, Mêne won particular approval from both French and English audiences for his scenes of domesticated animals, and deer and huntsman (fig. 10). The ranks of animalier sculptors expanded even further during the Second Empire to accommodate a broader and growing patronage.

These and other animaliers did not arouse the opposition of the art establishment as Barye did. In a way, the battle for the legitimacy of subject matter centered around Barye, perhaps because he was far more adventurous than his colleagues in selecting emotion-filled situations that involved wild animals. His complex, intricate groupings lacked the comfort of the familiar and thus confronted the viewer. In elevating this genre to a level comparable to the tradition of monumental sculpture, Barye was challenging the academic hierarchy of subject matter that had ruled French art since the seventeenth century.

# NOTES

I wish to express my gratitude to Dr. Edward J. Nygren for reviewing this essay and that on "Barye and Patronage." His constructive advice and criticism were invaluable. On behalf of the student contributors to this catalogue, I would also like to thank him for his guidance and indefatigable assistance in the research and writing of their essays.

1 Charles Blanc, *Les Artistes de Mon Temps* (Paris, 1876), 383–84.

2 Théophile Gautier, "Barye," *L'Illustration, Journal Universelle*, 19 (May 1866), 315.

3 "Antoine-Louis Barye," *Harper's New Monthly Magazine*, 71 (June-November 1885), 590.

4 Henry Eckford, "Antoine-Louis Barye," *Century Magazine*, 31, no. 4 (February 1886), 483–500.

5 That eclecticism has been identified not only in writings by nineteenth-century critics but also in contemporary studies of Barye. See, for example, Glenn F. Benge, *Antoine-Louis Barye: Sculptor of Romantic Realism* (University Park, PA, 1984), 9.

6 "Revue des Arts," *L'Artiste*, 1st ser., VIII (November 1834), 193.

7 Jacques Lethève, *Daily Life of French Artists in the Nineteenth Century*, trans. H. E. Paddon (New York, 1968), 132–33.

8 Joseph C. Sloane, *French Painting Between the Past and the Present* (Princeton, 1951), 23.

9 Kathrine B. Hiesinger and Joseph Rishel, "Art and Its Critics: A Crisis of Principle," in *The Second Empire, 1852–1870: Art in France under Napoleon III* (Philadelphia, 1978), 29.

10 Anne Pingeot, "Introduction," in *La Sculpture Française au XIXᵉ Siècle* (Paris, 1986), xiii, n. 6.

11 "Revue des Arts," *L'Artiste*, 1st ser., VIII (August 1834), 42–43.

12 "Sculpture," *The Second Empire*, 204.

13 Charles Avery, "From David d'Angers to Rodin: Britain's National Collection of French Nineteenth-Century Sculpture," *Studies in European Sculpture* (London, 1981), 261.

14 For a discussion of nineteenth-century sculptural theory and criticism, see Charles W. Millard, "Sculpture and Theory in Nineteenth-Century France," *Journal of Aesthetics and Art Criticism*, 34, no. 1 (Fall 1975), 15–20.

15 "Sculpture," *L'Artiste*, 1st ser., VIII (1834), 88.

16 *Ibid.*, 88–90.

17 Charles Baudelaire, "The Salon of 1846: Why Sculpture is Tiresome," *Baudelaire: Art in Paris, 1845–1862*, trans. J. Mayne (London, 1965), 112.

18 *Ibid.*

19 Pierre Malitourne, "La Sculpture en 1847," *L'Artiste*, 4th ser., IX (May 1847), 173.

20 Viollet-le-Duc, "L'Enseignement des Arts," *Gazette des Beaux-Arts*, 13 (July-September 1862), 254.

21 For a discussion of directions in nineteenth-century sculpture, see H. W. Janson, *Nineteenth-Century Sculpture* (New York, 1985) and *La Sculpture Française*.

22 Mailtourne, "La Sculpture en 1847," 171. See also W. C. Brownell, *French Art: Classic and Contemporary Painting and Sculpture* (New York, 1901), 157.

23 Baudelaire, "The Salon of 1846," 113.

24 See Gautier, "Barye," 315.

25 Although international in scope, this genre was dominated by French sculptors throughout the century. See Theodore Crombie, "French Animal Bronzes of the Nineteenth Century," *Connoisseur*, 151 (December 1962), 245–47.

26 While there was an interest in bronze during the seventeenth century in France, the metal was not used extensively until the following century. For further discussion, see George Savage, *A Concise History of Bronzes* (London, 1968).

27 For a discussion of the latter, see Isabella Leroy-Jay Lemaistre, "La Statuette Romantique," in *La Sculpture Française*, 260.

28 For a discussion of nineteenth-century bronze production, see Anthony Radcliffe, *European Bronze Statuettes* (London, 1966) and Jeremy Cooper, *Nineteenth-Century Romantic Bronzes* (Boston, 1975).

29 Saint-Chéron, "De la Décadence de l'Ecole des Beaux-Arts," *L'Artiste*, 1st ser., VIII (1834), 108.

30 An alternative to the private studio was study at the Petit Ecole, which served as a preparatory school in sculpture.

31 For a discussion of the system, see Anne Wagner, "Learning to Sculpt in the 19th Century," in *The Romantics to Rodin: French Nineteenth-Century Sculpture from North American Collections* (Los Angeles, 1980), 9–20.

32 The subjects assigned required a highly sophisticated artistic and cultural background. So demanding was the competition that some critics maintained that even experienced artists would falter. "Concours de Sculpture pour le Prix de Rome," *L'Artiste*, 1st ser., VIII (1834), 70.

33 Wagner, "Learning to Sculpt," 18.

34 In 1834, Barye and Antonin Moine were cited as such and praised as the only two artists of their generation who could be considered "real sculptors." *L'Artiste*, 1st ser., VIII (1834), 71.

35 Saint-Chéron, "De la Décadence," 108.

36 For a discussion of the reforms of the 1850s, see Clement de Ris, "Le Salon," *L'Artiste*, 5th ser., IV (January 1, 1851), 225–26. See also Albert Boime, "The Teaching Reforms of 1863 and the Origins of Modernism in France," *Art Quarterly*, 1 (Autumn 1977), 1–39.

37 "Sculpture," *The Second Empire*, 205.

38 See also Alfonz Lengyel, *Life and Art of Antoine-Louis Barye* (Dubuque, IA, 1963), 2–5.

39 Théophile Silvestre, *Les Artistes Français: études d'après nature* (Brussels, 1861), 119.

40 *Ibid.*, 120.

41 Although it was gradually being transformed, the officially sanctioned Classical style was rejected by the younger generation of Romantics. Associated with this group, Barye came to be viewed as a leading opponent of Classicism.

42 See also Benge, *Barye: Sculptor*, 3.

43 See A. Genevay, "A. L. Barye," *L'Art Revue hebdomadaire illustrée*, 2 (1875), 363–64, and Charles Clément, *Artistes Anciens et Modernes* (Paris, 1876), 395.

44 Genevay, "A. L. Barye," 365.

45 Blanc, *Les Artistes de Mon Temps*, 382.

46 T. H. E. Bements, "Barye's Sketchbook," *Scribner's Magazine*, 70 (July-December 1921), 251–56. See also Lengyel, *Life and Art*, 3, 18.

47 Charles Louis Borgmeyer, "Among Sculptures, Antoine L. Barye's (1796–1875)," *Fine Arts Journal*, 30 (June 1914), 280.

48 John Palmer Leeper, *Antoine-Louis Barye: 1796–1875* (San Antonio, TX, 1965), 1.

49 Silvestre, *Les Artistes Français*, 124–25.

50 "Antoine-Louis Barye," *Harper's New Monthly Magazine*, 590.

51 Lengyel, *Life and Art*, 5.

52 *Ibid.* For example, Frédéric Cuvier's *L'Histoire Naturelle des Mammifieres*, 1818.

53 Blanc, *Les Artistes de Mon Temps*, 382–84.

54 See Gustave Planche, "Peintres et Sculpteurs Modernes de la France," *Revue des Deux Mondes*, 3 (July 1851), 55. See also Benge, *Barye: Sculptor*, 13–16, for a detailed discussion of the piece.

55 "Antoine-Louis Barye," *Harper's New Monthly Magazine*, 590.

56 It was cast in bronze in 1832 and sold in 11- and 20-inch sizes in editions produced by Barye. Stuart Pivar, *The Barye Bronzes: A Catalogue Raisonné* (Woodbridge, Suffolk, 1974), 13.

57 "Antoine-Louis Barye," *Harper's New Monthly Magazine,* 585.

58 E. J. Delécluze, "Beaux-Arts, Exposition de 1831," *Journal des Débats* (May 25, 1831), 3. For another discussion of Delécluze's criticism and the response of the public, see Benge, *Barye: Sculptor,* 33.

59 Charles Clément, *Artistes Anciens et Modernes* (Paris, 1876), 396.

60 In introducing a contemporary genre subject in a vividly realistic manner and on a large scale, Rude was similarly presenting an alternative to works supported by the Ecole and the Academy.

61 They viewed themselves as "guardians of tradition . . . against innovation which might be a threat to principles they were so zealously guarding." Eugène Véron, "Exposition des oeuvres de Barye au Palais des Beaux-Arts," *L'Art,* 2, pt. 1 (November 22, 1876), 36.

62 For a discussion of French criticism, see Sloane, *French Painting Between Past and Present,* 23–87.

63 William Thompson Walters, comp., *Antoine-Louis Barye from the French of Various Critics* (Baltimore, 1885), 82.

64 Clément, *Artistes Anciens et Modernes,* 397.

65 These included sculptural contributions to such major monuments as the Arc de Triomphe and the Colonne de Juillet.

66 Théophile Silvestre, *Histoire des Artistes Vivants, Français et Etrangers, études d'après nature* (Paris, 1861), 201. Silvestre recorded that the sketches Barye produced while at Barbizon were of such quality that they astonished the sculptor's Barbizon friends. This group included Paul Huet, Camille Corot, Jules Dupré, and Théodore Rousseau.

67 Planche, "Peintres et Sculpteurs Modernes," 48.

68 *Ibid.,* 48–49. For a discussion of other aspects of Planche's criticism and the comments of other writers, see Benge, *Barye: Sculptor,* 35–36.

69 Planche, "Peintres et Sculpteurs Modernes," 48.

70 Charles Saunier, *Barye,* trans. Wilfred S. Jackson (New York, 1926), 25.

71 The latter was never realized and the former only partially.

72 "Antoine-Louis Barye," *Harper's New Monthly Magazine,* 592.

73 Borgmeyer, "Among Sculptures," 87.

74 "Barye," *Art Journal,* 50 (September 1888), 21–22.

75 Gautier, "Barye," 315.

76 Saunier, *Barye,* 29.

77 Blanc, *Les Artistes de Mon Temps,* 57.

78 Saunier, *Barye,* 61.

79 Prices ranged from 230 francs for an equestrian piece to 5 francs for a single small animal form. Saunier, *Barye,* 31.

80 It registered profits of 3,919 francs during the 1849–51 period. Benge, *Barye: Sculptor,* 163. See also Benge, 155–65, for an extensive discussion of the foundry enterprise and the partnership.

81 *Ibid.,* 156. That he was able to purchase them back for 35,000 francs is indicative of Barye's increasing affluence during the latter part of his career. His income in 1857 was approximately 62,000 francs. *Ibid.,* 156–57. This might be compared to the average income in 1860 of Parisians employed in lithographic printing, and haberdashery and lapidary businesses as well as in the manufacture of firearms, hardware, clocks, and silverware. Assuming a 60-hour work week for 50 weeks of the year at an average hourly rate of 1.5 francs, the annual salary can be calculated as 4,500 francs. For additional information and comparative analysis, see *Labor in Europe and America: A Special Report on the Rates of Wages, the Cost of Subsistence, and the Condition of the Working Classes in Great Britain, Germany, France, Belgium and other Countries of Europe; also in the United States and British America,* Washington, 1875.

82 Although the level of Barye's involvement was atypical in 1839, in later years other animalier sculptors participated in production. These included Pierre Jules Mêne, Emmanuel Fremiet, and Auguste Caine. See Jane Horswell, *Bronze Sculpture of 'Les Animaliers': Reference and Price Guide* (Clopton, England, 1971), ii.

83 "Antoine-Louis Barye," *Harper's New Monthly Magazine,* 595.

84 For further discussion, see Benge, *Barye: Sculptor,* 164.

85 See *ibid.,* 48.

86 For a discussion of his classical sources, see Glenn F. Benge, "Barye, Flaxman and Phidias," *Acts of the 24th International Congress of the History of Art,* 6 (Bologna, 1982), 99–105.

87 Benge, *Barye: Sculptor,* 6–7. Benge identifies four approaches in Barye's work after 1840.

88 Planche, "Peintres et Sculpteurs Modernes," 73.

89 *Ibid.*

90 Gérard Hubert, "Barye et la Critique de Son Temps," *Revue des Arts,* 6 (December 1956), 227.

91 Paul Mantz, "Artistes Contemporains: Barye," *Gazette des Beaux-Arts,* 2nd ser., I (1867), 123.

92 Gautier, "Barye," 35.

93 See Planche, "Peintres et Sculpteurs Modernes," 74.

94 Eckford, "Antoine-Louis Barye," 499.

95 Most notable among his champions were Théophile Gautier, Gustave Planche, Paul Mantz, Maxime du Camp, Charles Blanc, Charles Clément, and Léon Bonnat.

96 "Barye," *Art Journal,* 22.

97 Eckford, "Antoine-Louis Barye," 486.

98 Léon Bonnat, "Barye," *Gazette des Beaux-Arts,* 3rd ser., I (January-June 1889), 382.

99 For a discussion of these and other animalier sculptors, see Horswell, *Bronze Sculpture of 'Les Animaliers.'*

Fig. 11. *Seated Lion*.

# II

# Individuality

## BARYE'S AESTHETIC OF THE PARTICULAR

Elizabeth W. Harter, Laurence Pamer

Writing in 1890 in an early study of the artist, Roger Ballu remarked, "[Barye] knew the distinct characteristics of each race, the peculiarities of each species. No two of his animals are alike. Each has the individual aspect, pose and attitude proper to it—its own individuality. . . ."[1] This concern for individuality is especially evident in Barye's sculptures of single animals in conventional poses. Each animal is particular in detail but general in its presentation. With few exceptions, Barye's works are depictions of generic types rather than portraits of specific animals.[2]

Barye began to model single animals in the 1820s. He created many new images in the 1830s, which he continued to produce throughout his life. These sculptures account for more than one-quarter of his total output of over three hundred models.[3] For the most part, these statues of single animals were small and thus suited to the residences and budgets of the nineteenth-century French middle class. Subjects range from domestic dogs to stalking panthers. The majority, however, represent undomesticated species, such as lions, deer, bears, birds, rabbits, and elephants. More than a third of Barye's objects in the Corcoran's collection feature single animals. Totaling thirty-seven works in all, these examples are indicative of the artist's output in this genre.

Among Barye's many subjects, deer, bears, canines, horses, and wild felines prevail. Depictions of these beasts share several characteristics. Although the animals usually represented are untame, they appear calmer and more benign than when the same creatures are presented in hunting scenes or confrontations. In a clear departure from those dramatic groups, some of the single subjects, such as *Seated Bear* (fig. 12), are touched with humor. Moreover, each sculpture concentrates on character, mood, and emotion to project the individuality of the beast.

Barye portrayed felines more frequently than any other animal. Representations of a solitary lion, tiger, jaguar, or panther number at least thirty, with the lion being the most commonly treated. The sculptor had ample opportunity to study these animals in the Jardin des Plantes and in traveling circuses. Occasionally, Barye participated in dissections and made detailed anatomical drawings of his observations.[4]

He was undoubtedly aware of the representation of the lion in western art from antiquity to his own day. A noble beast of awesome strength, the lion frequently symbolized royalty in art and heraldry. The Corcoran's collection contains four freestanding examples of lions: *Lioness of Senegal, Lioness of Algiera, Walking Lion,* and *Seated Lion.* Of the four, *Seated Lion* (fig. 11) is perhaps the best known since it is a reduction of a monumental work that today flanks one of the entrances to the Louvre. It also epitomizes Barye's ability to capture the nobility of the species without losing a sense of the creature's individuality. The quiet but alert pose with head held high conveys the general majesty and vigilance of the lion, while the hunched shoulders, aged face, and detailed rendering of the mane express the subject's individuality. Such emphasis on mood and scientific accuracy signaled a significant change from the stylized lions of earlier periods, when manes "resembled

Fig. 12. *Seated Bear.*

the wigs of the Louis XIV style."[5]

Louis-Philippe commissioned Barye to create the life-size version of *Seated Lion,* now outside the Louvre, for the Tuileries Gardens. Cast in 1847, it was installed in 1848, the year the king was overthrown.[6] In two earlier sculptures—*Lion Crushing a Serpent* (fig. 4) and *Lion of the Column of July* (fig. 13)—Barye depicted the lion as a symbol of the July Monarchy. *Lion Crushing a Serpent* has been interpreted as symbolizing the ascension of

Louis-Philippe following the Revolution of 1830, which occurred in July, the month astrologically dominated by Leo. Further reinforcing the astrological symbolism associated with the revolution is *Lion of the Column of July,* a reduction of the relief created for the monument erected in the Place de la Bastille to honor those killed in the Revolution of 1830.[7] In contrast, *Seated Lion* reflects a tradition dating to the *Lion Gate of Mycenae* (ca. 1250 B.C.) in its suggestion of a quiet guardian of the State.

Fig. 13. *Lion of the Column of July.*

Barye's interest in equine subjects resulted in at least seven different versions of the single horse. Horses were, of course, an essential element of nineteenth-century life since they were used for labor, transportation, and entertainment. At the Parisian horse markets, Barye had the opportunity to study the horse and sketch a variety of breeds.[8] His choice of subjects ranges from the domestic mule, Percheron, and half-blood horse to the untamed Arabian and Turkish horse.

Although several of Barye's single horses appear relaxed, the figure of the *Turkish Horse* (fig. 14) is wildly agitated. Like his compatriot Eugène Delacroix, Barye may have found in the fiery Turkish horse an expression of the Romantic spirit.[9] Pawing the ground and lowering its head, the animal apparently reacts to an unseen antagonist. In this manner, Barye both heightened the emotional tension of the moment and implied the development of a narrative, letting the viewer construct the scene. The Corcoran's collection includes two versions of *Turkish Horse,* one raising its right foreleg, the other, its left. *Half-Blood Horse* (fig. 15) is the only other single equine subject in the collection.

Deer were also frequent subjects for Barye; he created sculptures of single deer at least twenty-five times. His exploration of the subject was probably encouraged by French enthusiasm for deer hunting, for one of the most highly prized trophies was the mounted head or antlers of a stag. Barye was specific in his delineation of deer breeds: in addition to stags, does, and fawns, he portrayed the Java, Axis, Ganges, and Virginia deer. In Barye's rendering of the four breeds, the Ganges deer

Fig. 14. *Turkish Horse.*

Fig. 15. *Half-Blood Horse, with Head Down.*

Fig. 16. *Virginia Deer Reclining.*

has the thickest and longest coat and the Virginia deer the shortest. Other distinguishing characteristics of the Virginia deer are its ears, which are larger than those of the others, and its antlers, which curve forward, while those of the other three breeds grow backwards and project farther away from the head. Barye may have noted these variations at the Jardin des Plantes or in the natural histories available during the nineteenth century, such as those written by Baron George Cuvier and Count Buffon, which were known to him.[10]

Barye shows the single deer in realistic settings engaged in characteristic activities—braying, reclining, walking, listening, or rubbing its antlers against a tree. Eight versions of the deer belong to the Corcoran, including *Virginia Deer Reclining* (fig. 16), in which the animal is simply shown either scratching or cleaning itself. Glenn F. Benge likens Barye's deer to the animals in the natural history diorama that Barye probably saw at the Jardin des Plantes.[11]

Single canines are represented at least sixteen times in Barye's *oeuvre*, five examples of which are in the Corcoran's collection. Depictions of wolves, spaniels, bassets, pointers, and greyhounds, as well as sculptures identified simply as "dog," comprise this category. Barye undoubtedly studied canine anatomy during his visits to the Parisian dog markets or by observing his pet greyhound Tom (fig. 20), one of the few animals recorded as having been kept by the sculptor.[12] Even though most of the single canines Barye sculpted are hunting dogs, which suggests he had a particular audience in mind, their hunting instincts are not usually

emphasized. Some stand or sit quietly, as if to accentuate their domesticated nature. For example, in *English Basset* (fig. 17), the dog's eager glance and the apparent wag of its tail evoke a tender mood that is strikingly different from the qualities displayed in the hounds of the hunt groups (see fig. 26).

Barye's skill at recreating canine anatomy is particularly apparent in *Tom, Algerian Greyhound* (fig. 20). The dog's pronounced rib cage and the rippling hide that covers it attest to the sculptor's proficiency, as does the

Fig. 17. *English Basset.*

20

Fig. 19. *Standing Bear.*

expert depiction of tension in the dog's haunches. Such anatomical details reveal that Barye "concentrated not only on the exterior of the animal, . . . but also on the interior as it related itself to the exterior."[13]

Of all the animals Barye treated repeatedly, the bear was the most unusual. It has been noted that "Barye . . . surprised the world by deigning to employ his acknowledged talent as a sculptor in modeling a thoroughly unfashionable, an almost ridiculous beast."[14] Although a bear has astronomical and heraldic meaning, the lumbering animal appeared infrequently in western art except in hunting scenes or as an entertainment. For Barye, the bear was an exotic animal with spirit and sentiment. Although the sculptor would have seen bears in the Jardin des Plantes as well as in circuses and street performances, there were also more personal associations with the creature. For instance, the name "Barye," as DeKay suggests, may have derived from a form of the word "bear."[15] Additionally, a contemporary caricaturist noticed a physical resemblance between Barye and a bear, and in an amusing illustration alluded both to this coincidence and to Barye's treatment of this uncommon subject (fig. 18).

During the nineteenth-century, zoologists assigned dozens of names of species to bears. In his demand for

Fig. 18. Unknown. *Pantheon Charivarique—Barye,* from *Charivari.* Lithograph. George A. Lucas Collection of The Maryland Institute, College of Art, on indefinite loan to The Baltimore Museum of Art.

scientific accuracy, Barye followed their practice, giving his sculptures geographical designations such as Russian, Alpine, North American, and Indian. Due to Barye's study of bears at the Jardin des Plantes, one author notes that the subjects read like plaques on the cages.[16] Also, Barye treated the single bear almost as a domestic animal, showing it as it was in captivity, not in the wild.

*Fig. 20. Tom, Algerian Greyhound.*

Barye's *oeuvre* contains seven depictions of single bears, two of which are in the Corcoran's collection: *Standing Bear* (fig. 19) and *Seated Bear* (fig. 12), both from the early 1830s. Projecting a humanlike nature, the bulky proportions evident in *Standing Bear* are made more noticeable by the animal's awkward stance on its hind legs. One short leg steps forward, the front paws reach out for balance, and the face gazes directly at the viewer. Although comparable in its proportions, narrow long snout, and thick ruff of fur, *Seated Bear* displays both a sketchier technique and a more playful attitude. Barye's sentimentalized sculptures of these animals elicit an almost childlike delight from the viewer analogous to the response of visitors observing the antics of bears at the Jardin des Plantes. Similar to his depictions of other single animals, Barye invested his bears with character, mood, and emotion to project their individuality.

## NOTES

1   Roger Ballu, "Antoine-Louis Barye," in *Masters in Art: A Series of Illustrated Monographs,* vol. 5 (Boston, 1904), 409. This excerpt is a translation from Roger Ballu, *L'Oeuvre de Barye* (Paris, 1890).

2   Barye even refers to a "cheval de race" in his lengthy description of a horse in a manuscript preserved at the Ecole des Beaux-Arts. An exception is *Tom, Algerian Greyhound* (fig. 20), discussed below.

3   Barye often produced more than one size of cast for a single model. Multiple copies then could be manufactured according to demand. The most comprehensive list of Barye's models for bronze sculptures appears in Stuart Pivar, *The Barye Bronzes: A Catalogue Raisonné* (Woodbridge, Suffolk, 1974).

4   Barye studied the lion's anatomy with his friend Eugène Delacroix; see M. François-Raphaël Loffredo, "Des Recherches Communes de Barye et de Delacroix au Laboratoire d'Anatomie Comparée Musée d'Histoire Naturelle," *Bulletin de la Société de l'Histoire de l'Art Français* (December 1982), 147.

5   A comment attributed to Théophile Gautier in Charles Sprague Smith, *Barbizon Days* (1902; rpt., Freeport, 1969), 202.

6   The sculpture was moved to the quai-side portal of the Flore Pavilion, Louvre Palace, in 1867. A reversed mechanical copy was created as a companion piece without Barye's permission, according to Charles DeKay, *Barye: Life and Works of Antoine-Louis Barye, Sculptor* (1889; rpt. New York, 1974)), 70.

7   Images of lions also appeared as tomb decorations in classical tradition, so the lion was particularly appropriate to commemorate those who had died. Glenn F. Benge, *Antoine-Louis Barye: Sculptor of Romantic Realism* (University Park, PA, 1984), 38.

8   T. H. E. Bements, "Barye's Sketchbook," *Scribner's Magazine,* 70 (July-December 1921), 255.

9   Frank Anderson Trapp, *The Attainment of Delacroix* (Baltimore, 1971), 218.

10   Eugène Guillaume, "Introduction," in Roger Ballu, *L'Oeuvre de Barye* (Paris, 1890), xxiii. These natural histories also may have prompted Barye's differentiation among the breeds of bears, canines, equines, and felines. See Baron George Cuvier, *The Animal Kingdom,* trans. H. M. Murtrie (New York, 1831); and George Louis Leclerc, Count de Buffon, *Histoire Naturelle, Générale et Particulière, avec la Description du Cabinet du Roi* (44 vols.; Paris, 1750–1804).

11   Benge, *Barye: Sculptor,* 19.

12   *Ibid.,* 3; Pivar, *Barye Bronzes,* 18. Pivar writes that in 1868, in an exception to Barye's practice of depicting generic types, the sculptor created a marble, lifesize portrait of Tom to fulfill a commission. The author also reproduces the 1865 catalogue in which "Tom, lévrier d'Algérie" appears under "Nouveaux Modeles." The measurements of this sculpture correspond almost exactly with those of the Corcoran's greyhound, while other greyhound sculptures do not. Thus, it is reasonable to assume that the title of this particular bronze subject from the Corcoran's collection is the one given in the 1865 catalogue, since that catalogue was the basis for the purchases made by Walters for the Corcoran.

13   Alfonz Lengyel, *Life and Art of Antoine-Louis Barye* (Dubuque, 1A, 1963), 1.

14   DeKay, *Life and Works,* 46.

15   *Ibid.,* 45.

16   Pivar, *Barye Bronzes,* 15. Today's natural histories identify eight species of bear in the world, none of which Barye named specifically. Nineteenth-century scientific works considered local geographical variations of bear to be entirely separate species.

# Barye's

## EXOTIC HUNT SCENES

Barbara J. Stephanic

The Corcoran's collection of Barye's animal sculpture includes three pieces in which the animal allies with man and the pursuit of prey becomes the sport of the hunt. The Corcoran's hunt pieces are *Indian Mounted on an Elephant Crushing a Tiger* (fig. 21), in which an elephant with an Indian rider engages a tiger in combat; *Two Arab Horsemen Killing a Lion* (fig. 23), in which a horseman spears a lion while a second who holds a gun recovers from a fall; and *North African Horseman Surprised by a Serpent* (fig. 25), in which a monstrous snake crushes both a horse and its rider. All three works depict scenes from exotic parts of the world.

The long tradition of the hunt in art goes back to antiquity. Lion hunts appear on Mesopotamian relief sculptures and Roman sarcophagi, and in medieval tapestries and paintings by Rubens. Numerous illustrated books on the hunt were published from the sixteenth century on. In the nineteenth century, specific volumes were even devoted to Oriental sports.[1]

Within Barye's *oeuvre,* the theme of the hunt appears early in his career. A commission in 1834 for a colossal table decoration from the Duke of Orléans, eldest son of Louis-Philippe, afforded Barye not only a challenge but also the opportunity to explore further his interest in animal subjects and to represent animals in exotic settings. The pieces for the *surtout de table* included men with animals as well as animal confrontations and thus addressed the theme of the hunt on a variety of levels.[2]

Elaborate suites, such as the *surtout,* which could include a complete flatware service, candelabra, jardinières, ornamental dishes, and centerpieces, had been produced for the nobility and the wealthy since the Middle Ages. These ornate ensembles were usually ordered from silversmiths. For example, the famed French silversmith of the nineteenth century, Charles Christofle, produced in 1865 an ensemble of 4,938 pieces for Emperor Maxmilian of Mexico. Reputedly designed to be more lavish than a similar *surtout* created for the Empress Eugènie, it was exhibited in the Salon before it was delivered to Mexico.[3] While Barye's *surtout* stemmed from this tradition of table decoration, the theme of the hunt and the integration of exotic animals with human figures was his own conception.

This commission, however, was never fully realized. Its initial plan called for an ensemble of fifteen hunt or animal groups to be arranged among an array of towers, temples, arcades, and colonnades. Each segment was to consist of animals, hunting paraphernalia, and costumes representative of a particular part of the world. Individual pieces were to be cast in silver or gold, and encrusted with precious stones. The entire assemblage was to span twenty-one feet in length and be displayed on a special table designed to hold the *surtout*'s massive weight.[4] The project, which proved too costly for the duke, was abandoned four years later, in 1838. By then Barye had cast in bronze the five large hunt groups intended for the central pieces and four of the small animal confrontations.

Barye's interest in the Orient emerges in the works for the *surtout* as well as in the variations on the hunt theme that he subsequently created in bronze and watercolor. He was drawn to exotic subjects through the

Fig. 21. *Indian Mounted on an Elephant Crushing a Tiger.*

works of contemporary writers and artists. Romantic images of harems, baths, and odalisques were popularized by writers such as Baudelaire, Flaubert, and Gerard de Nerval. Painters such as Jean-Léon Gérôme, Eugène Fromentin, and Eugène Delacroix exhibited works at the Salon celebrating the rich colors, textures, and architecture of North Africa and the Near East.

Although the Corcoran owns none of the pieces produced specifically for the *surtout,* the three works mentioned above, as well as *Bear Fleeing from Dogs* (fig. 26), are strongly dependent in both subject matter and style on the groups created for the duke. *Indian Mounted on an Elephant Crushing a Tiger* (fig. 21), for example, is derived from *Tiger Hunt* (fig. 22), the principal center-

24

piece of the *surtout*. Both depict the Indian *mahout*, a professional elephant handler, seated in a *howdah* at the moment of confrontation between an elephant and a tiger. The Corcoran piece is a simpler version of *Tiger Hunt*, with only one rider on an elephant.[5] Barye treated this same theme on other occasions. A plaster and wax model of an elephant that stands erect and strides foward with a single rider can be found in the Louvre.[6] The Corcoran piece, however, is a closer variation of the work in the *surtout*. It is also possible that Barye's undated watercolors of related subjects were executed about the same time as the *surtout*.[7]

Barye is specific in his rendering of an Asiatic elephant in *Indian Mounted on an Elephant Crushing a Tiger*. Indigenous to the region that extends east from the Indian subcontinent to China, the Asian elephant is somewhat smaller than that of Africa or China and is further distinguished by its small ears and bulging fore-head. Since an elephant in the wild would not initiate an attack on a tiger, it had to be trained to corner its predator and provoke a confrontation. The hunter would then make the kill from the safe position atop the elephant, which is the moment depicted here.

Contemporary prints or paintings as well as journal accounts of Indian nobility and their use of the elephant may have served as reference sources for Barye. From a notation in one of Barye's sketchbooks, George Heard Hamilton identified one such source as a volume of portraits of Moghul emperors of India compiled by Niccolao Manucci, first published in 1705. A copy of the French translation entered the Bibliothèque Nationale in 1797.[8] As Hamilton points out, Barye's depiction of the elephant resembles an engraving in Manucci's book of Emperor Akbar riding atop an elephant, both in complete royal regalia.[9]

Barye's composition follows the Manucci illustration

**Fig. 22.** *Tiger Hunt*. Walters Art Gallery, Baltimore.

closely, yet the scene would be unlikely to occur in nature. Although Barye's elephant is anatomically correct, its pose is awkward for an animal in combat. It appears as if the elephant is resting rather than fighting. Moreover, an elephant possesses a natural sensitivity in its trunk, the only means by which it can feed itself. In combat it typically holds its trunk aloft and out of reach of an antagonist. It is also improbable that the elephant would tuck its front leg under itself, a movement that would force its huge weight to roll to one side and thus leave the animal vulnerable to attack.

Another component of the *surtout, Lion Hunt* (fig. 24), relates to the Corcoran's *Two Arab Horsemen Killing a Lion* (fig. 23). Barye rendered the dramatic scene convincingly as he portrayed the majestic lion struggling against its inevitable defeat. This piece, while a simpler composition than that of the *surtout,* shows the artist's

concern for distinctive characteristics and detailed accuracy. For example, the saddle, bridle, and harness are particular to Arabic culture, as are the headdress and robes of the two horsemen. The billowing robes of the mounted Arab, along with the swirling movement of the horse, powerfully express energetic activity.

The third Corcoran sculpture to deal with the hunt is *North African Horseman Surprised by a Serpent* (fig. 25). In this depiction of predator and prey, the serpent triumphs as the horse and rider become its victims. Although the serpent is an heraldic device and an astrological sign, in religion, mythology, and folklore it most commonly symbolizes evil. In *Lion Crushing a Serpent* (fig. 4), Barye associated the snake with the accession of the July Monarchy of Louis-Philippe in 1830.[10] He also created a number of works in watercolor and bronze in which the serpent appears as one of the com-

Fig. 24. *Lion Hunt*. Walters Art Gallery, Baltimore.

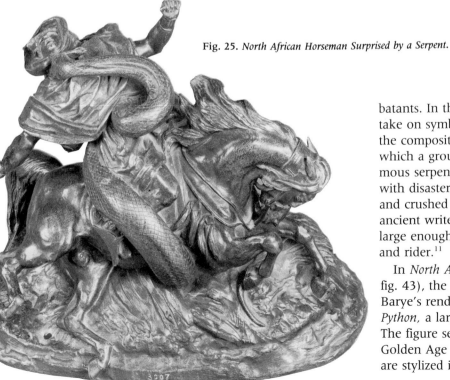

Fig. 25. *North African Horseman Surprised by a Serpent.*

batants. In these works, the serpent does not seem to take on symbolic significance. Glenn F. Benge suggests the composition may deal with a story from antiquity in which a group of hunters were sent to capture an enormous serpent for the amusement of the king. They met with disaster when the serpent swallowed one hunter and crushed another in its coils. In the story by the ancient writer Diodorus, the serpent was described as large enough to raise its head into the air above a horse and rider.[11]

In *North African Horseman Surprised by a Serpent* (see fig. 43), the face and head of the rider relate closely to Barye's rendering of the figure in *Greek Rider Seized by a Python*, a large, ca. 1835 plaster model in the Louvre.[12] The figure seems to be a combination of Archaic and Golden Age Greek styles. Although his hair and beard are stylized in the Archaic manner, he lacks the smile

27

Fig. 26. *Bear Fleeing from Dogs.*

and almond-shaped eyes of the earlier style. Moreover, the rider's facial features are reminiscent of the fearful expression of the Trojan priest Laocoön in the famous Hellenistic sculptural group. (Barye may have known the original and would certainly have seen a copy of the famed sculpture in the Tuileries.)[13]

It is important to note that these works are not isolated examples of Barye's reference to the pieces in the *surtout*. For example, *Bear Fleeing from Dogs* (fig. 26), which probably dates from 1855 to 1865, is a variation on an element from the *Bear Hunt* (see fig. 55).[14] The bear in each piece fends off the attack of hounds. This work illustrates how Barye returned, after twenty years, to the *surtout* for inspiration. Like other exotic hunt scenes, it provides evidence of the importance of the *surtout de table* throughout Barye's career.

## NOTES

1  William A. Baillie-Grohman, *Sport in Art: An Iconography of Sport from the Fifteenth to the End of the Eighteenth Century* (London, 1919) is a seminal study of the subject. Among nineteenth-century illustrated volumes devoted to pastimes in exotic places, one of the most ambitious was Captain Thomas Williamson, *Oriental Field Sports* (London, 1808) in two volumes with hand-colored engravings, including a series dealing with a tiger hunt by Samuel Howitt. The titles of the illustrations were given in French as well as English, indicating the desire to reach an international market.

2  For a discussion of the five principle pieces of the original nine groups in the *surtout de table*, see William R. Johnston, "The Barye Collection of the Walters Art Gallery, Baltimore," *Apollo*, 50 (November 1974), 402–409.

3  For an illustration of one of the jardinières, see *The Second Empire, 1852–1870: Art in France Under Napoleon III* (Philadelphia, 1978), 129.

4  The architect Aimé Chenavard was commissioned to design an elaborately decorated table for the *surtout*. See Roger Ballu, *L'Oeuvre de Barye* (Paris, 1890), 56–58.

5  For a discussion of the central *Tiger Hunt* scene, see George Heard Hamilton, "The Origin of Barye's Tiger Hunt," *Art Bulletin* 18 (June, 1936), 249–59.

6  For an illustration of the Louvre piece, see Hamilton, *ibid.*, 250, and Stuart Pivar, *The Barye Bronzes: A Catalogue Raisonné* (Woodbridge, Suffolk, 1974), 65.

7  Examples of Barye's watercolors of the *Tiger Hunt* are in both the Corcoran's and the Walters' collections. See Martina Norelli, "The Watercolors of Antoine-Louis Barye," elsewhere in this catalogue.

8  The French translation of *Storia do Mogor by Niccolao*, 1705, documents eyewitness accounts of Moghul India, 1628–80. See Hamilton, "The Origin of Barye's Tiger Hunt," 253.

9  See the English translation of *Storia do Mogor by Niccolao*, translated by William Irving, fig. VIII, for an illustration of the emperor riding atop an elephant. It was originally published in Manucci's volume of portraits of 1797. Hamilton also illustrates this comparison in "The Origin of Barye's Tiger Hunt," 258, fig. 9.

10  See Glenn F. Benge, *Antoine-Louis Barye: Sculptor of Romantic Realism* (University Park, PA, 1984), 3.

11  This story by Diodordus was published in French translation in 1834. See Benge, *ibid.*, 98–99, 101. For the full story in English translation see *Diodorus of Sicily*, trans. C. H. Oldfather (12 vols.; Cambridge, MA, 1967). Benge discusses the popularity of the publication *Bibliotheca historia* and considers the story a specific source for this piece.

12  See Benge, *Barye: Sculptor*, 108, for a comparison of these works as well as a drawing of *Python Attacking a Horseman*.

13  Barye may well have seen the original sculpture prior to its return to Rome in 1816, the same year he entered the studio of François Bosio. See Francis Haskell and Nicholas Penny, *Taste and the Antique* (New Haven, 1981), 243.

14  See Benge, *Barye: Sculptor*, 131.

# IV

# Barye's

## DRAMAS OF ANIMAL PASSIONS

Edward J. Nygren

In *Cousin Bette*, set in Paris during the late 1830s, Balzac remarks:

> Sculpture is like Drama; at once more difficult and easier than all the other arts. One can copy a model and the work is done; but to impart a soul to it, in the representing of a man or woman to create a type, is to snatch fire from heaven like Prometheus. Sculptors who have succeeded in this area are rare and glorious landmarks in human history.[1]

The author's comparison is particularly relevant to the work of Barye, whose confrontations are, as one contemporary critic observed, "little dramas so simple, yet deep in effect."[2] The purpose of this essay is to examine how Barye used the natural dramas of animal life to project an emotional attitude that transcends the anecdotal. Just as Balzac, whose novels Barye admired,[3] presented a "natural history of human society in which the different social classes would correspond to the different zoological species,"[4] the sculptor created a series of animal histories which correspond to human experience.

Among the more than three hundred works in Barye's sculptural *oeuvre*, two-thirds are animal subjects. Animals predominate, singly or in groups, in various activities or moods, as predator or prey. Of the approximately two hundred animal bronzes, more than half are hunting scenes or confrontations.[5] The Corcoran's collection reflects this general division. Over a third of the one hundred works owned by the museum represent life-and-death struggles.

Barye's animal dramas are of three basic types: mythological combats that include man; hunting scenes, in which man appears or his presence is implied by a sur-rogate, such as a hound; and confrontations between savage predators and their prey. The focus of this paper is the last category.[6] Battles between wild animals first brought Barye recognition, and they remain central to his enduring reputation.

The mature period of Barye's career is bracketed by key treatments of animal confrontations. At the Salon of 1831, he received attention for *Tiger Devouring a Gavial* (fig. 27). Two years later *Lion Crushing a Serpent* (fig. 31) brought him his first major State commission. In the Salon of 1850–51, he reemerged with *Jaquar Devouring a Hare* (fig. 36). Before 1831, between 1837 and 1850, and after 1850, many variations on the confrontation theme were produced. Although the creation of a specific work cannot always be dated with pinpoint accuracy, most pieces were conceived during those prolific two decades when the sculptor forged a personal style and exploited a subject matter that became synonymous with his name.

From the 1820s on, Barye was an avid student of anatomy. Throughout most of his life, he made extensive studies at the Jardin des Plantes and at the Museum of Natural History, where he spent the last twenty years of his life teaching anatomical drawing. Alone or with his friend Eugène Delacroix, Barye dissected animals and made meticulous measured drawings of specimens.[7]

Barye belonged to a scientific community that centered on the Museum of Natural History. The brothers George and Frédéric Cuvier and Etienne Geoffroy Saint-Hilaire numbered among his associates. He was familiar with Count Buffon's monumental *Natural History* and reportedly was much influenced by Frédéric Cuvier's observations on animal instinct and intelligence.[8] Founded in 1793, the library at the Museum of Natural History contained natural histories, dictionaries, travel accounts, and monographs on animals, which provided Barye with information and inspiration.[9]

Although Barye used his studies of animal anatomy to develop a naturalistic style, he was not interested in anatomy or natural history for their own sake. As one contemporary noted, Barye was not a pure naturalist.[10] He did not, for example, reproduce nature as he knew it, having never personally observed the confrontations he depicted. Occasionally the sculptor pitted animals against each other which did not coexist geographically or were not natural enemies. He also distorted features to convey the feelings of his subjects and to define their character, good or evil.[11] His animal engagements, so full of passion and drama, were products of a creative, Romantic imagination, not presentations of scientific conclusions.

Barye's approach to his subject was not solely shaped by his anatomical studies at the Jardin des Plantes or his

attention to Barye as a sculptor were *Tiger Devouring a Crocodile* [*sic*], *Lion Crushing a Serpent, Stag Brought Down by Hounds* and *Horse Attacked by a Lion.*" He went on to say, "I do not know what the public thought of these works, but all the artists of the new school [Romanticism] were astonished and enraptured. They found there what they had vainly sought in the works of their elders, the true perception of life, of truth, of liberty."[13] (All these works, which date from the early 1830s, are represented in the Corcoran's collection.)[14]

*Tiger Devouring a Gavial* (fig. 27) deals with two exotic beasts. The gavial is an unusual type of crocodile, and Barye was undoubtedly familiar with recently published studies on this creature, a skeleton of which is preserved in the Museum of Natural History.[15] Although there were no live tigers in Paris until Henry Martin's menageries visited the city in August of 1829, the Museum owned stuffed specimens. A Bengal tiger was acquired by the Jardin des Plantes in August of 1830, and perhaps this event was the catalyst for Barye's sculpture.[16]

This piece, which won a second prize at the Salon, established Barye's reputation. At the time of its exhibition, Delécluze remarked in *Journal des Débats*:

Fig. 27. *Tiger Devouring a Gavial.*

research at the Museum of Natural History. Artistic sources for specific scenes have been identified. Compositions such as *Horse Attacked by a Lion* (fig. 28) and *Rearing Bull with Tiger* claim a long visual tradition dating to antiquity. From the Renaissance on, numerous illustrated books as well as prints, paintings, sculptures, and the decorative arts had dealt with the theme of animal confrontations and the hunt. Barye knew and utilized these various sources.[12]

Writing on the occasion of Barye's retrospective at the Ecole des Beaux-Arts following the sculptor's death, Charles Blanc remarked, "The first works which drew

The tiger hugging the crocodile [*sic*] in his paws, and this reptile in fear and agony doubling on himself, form a group so true, so dreadful that it is difficult to withdraw your attention once fixed upon it. And although the beings here represented belong to a lower creation, *life* is rendered with such force and passion in these two animals, that we do not hesitate to pronounce the group which they form, the strongest and best work of sculpture in the Salon.[17]

Similar sentiments were expressed in other journals of the day.

Formidable antagonists, the tiger and gavial were creatures that arouse fear, not sympathy, in the viewer. Both were characterized in contemporary literature as

Fig. 28. *Horse Attacked by a Lion.*

depraved and evil. The naturalist Buffon and the physiognomist Johann Caspar Lavater spoke at length about the base character of the tiger and how it delights in blood, glutting itself until intoxicated. In *Tiger Devouring a Gavial*, Barye visualized what Buffon described as the tiger's brutal practice of tearing its prey for no other purpose than to plunge its head into the body.[18]

Here, the composition is a variation on *Tiger Attacking a Stag* of 1830 (fig. 29), but the psychological content of the two dramas is quite different. The bent neck and open mouth of the deer, whose legs are tucked painfully beneath its body, emphasize the intense anguish and cruel death of a gentle animal. In *Tiger Devouring a Gavial*, the awesome life-and-death struggle of two vicious creatures commands attention. Even though the earlier work is more affecting, it also treats a conventional theme, one that Barye explored several times. In *Tiger Devouring a Gazelle* and *Tiger Attacking an Antelope* (fig. 30), as well as in *Tiger Attacking a Stag*, the cat passionately embraces its victim, its mouth clamped in a vampirish kiss on the graceful neck of its swooning prey.[19]

The drama and passion of *Tiger Devouring a Gavial* was generally admired, even while the wealth of detail in the tiger's coat and the rich vegetation was criticized.[20] Not evident in the Corcoran's reduction, such details enliven the cast at the Louvre as they impart a lifelike quality to the image. The vignette of a turtle trying to get out from under the gavial introduces an anecdotal incident to the demonic struggle.

Fig. 29. *Tiger Attacking a Stag.*

Fig. 30. *Tiger Attacking an Antelope.*

Although Barye was credited with having invented this unusual subject,[21] *Tiger Devouring a Gavial* and *Lion Crushing a Serpent* (fig. 31) of 1833, like other works from the period, may owe a debt to British art.[22] A confrontation between a tiger and a crocodile as well as one between a lion and a serpent were painted by James Northcote around 1800, and the compositions were engraved. Northcote's treatment of a tiger and a crocodile looking warily at each other bear little resemblance to Barye's group, yet it could have inspired the sculptor to undertake the subject. The theme of the lion and serpent is another matter. Northcote's composition (fig. 32) so closely parallels Barye's allegory on the July Monarchy[23] that there can be little doubt that the sculptor was familiar with this print and, therefore, possibly with other works by the Englishman.[24]

In *Lion Crushing a Serpent*, the viewer's sympathy is with the cat. We share the lion's anger and perhaps fear of what was universally considered the vilest of creatures and laud its victory over the embodiment of evil incarnate.[25] Barye's treatment of the lion, here as elsewhere, emphasizes the beast's nobility and magnanimity. At the time it was widely believed that this member of the cat family killed only to survive. The lion's behavior was contrasted with the malevolence and cruelty of the tiger, who killed out of blood-thirsty love of gore.[26] Delacroix, for example, used the lion to

symbolize heroic man, and the tiger, human vice.[27] And although Barye occasionally depicted the lion with its victim, as in *Lion Devouring a Doe* or *Horse Attacked by a Lion* (fig. 28), the sculptor did not generally stress the predatory nature of the king of beasts.[28]

Fig. 32. Samuel W. Reynolds after James Northcote, *Lion and Snake.* Mezzotint with engraving. Yale Center for British Art, Paul Mellon Collection.

Fig. 33. *Python Killing a Gnu*. Walters Art Gallery, Baltimore.

The original bronzes of *Tiger Devouring a Gavial* and *Lion Crushing a Serpent* (figs. 2, 4) at the Louvre project an intensity that is noticeably absent from Northcote's conceptions and from the small versions owned by the Corcoran. Contributing to their effectiveness are the sheer physical presence of the originals and their tactile and sensual qualities. Unlike their printed counterparts or the reductions, these large bronzes vicariously involve the viewer in the action by forcing him to examine the piece from different points of view in order to experience it completely. Thus, the viewer psychologically becomes the predator, and the sculpture, his prey.

Among Barye's most startling images are his gigantic serpents devouring creatures, a subject he treated in both bronze and watercolor. *Python Killing a Gnu* (fig. 33) was one of the subsidiary pieces in the *surtout de table* created for the Duke of Orléans. Other sculptures of similar subjects probably date from this same period, especially *Python Crushing a Gazelle* (fig. 34), a variation on the former work. Both *Python Crushing a Crocodile*

Fig. 34. *Python Crushing a Gazelle*.

(fig. 35) and *Python Swallowing a Doe*,[29] the latter dated 1840, are thematically related, as is *North African Horseman Surprised by a Serpent* (fig. 25). Barye also painted a number of confrontations between large snakes and other animals.[30]

Unlike *Lion Crushing a Serpent*, these representations are probably not politically symbolic. The subject of enormous predatory snakes derives from the *Laocoön*. Until the rediscovery of that famous Hellenistic work in the early sixteenth century, little artistic attention had been paid to the theme. From the seventeenth century on, natural histories and travel accounts confirmed the existence of such beasts and recounted tales of confrontations between reptiles and other animals. Many of these books were illustrated, often with fanciful images.

Barye's interest in the subject coincides with the Jardin des Plantes' acquisition of two pythons from Java in 1836. The arrival of these reptiles and of three alligators from New Orleans marked the beginning of the Ménagerie des Reptiles.[31] A 1797 French translation of J. G. Stedman's *Voyage to Surinam*, owned by George Cuvier and containing an illustration of a huge serpent, entered the library of the Museum of Natural History in 1837. Moreover, the library also had a dictionary of natural history that was intended for artists, which gave a long description of the boa constrictor and its ability to devour alive large quadrupeds, such as deer, gazelles, bulls, tigers, and lions, as well as men.[32]

The sculptor's treatments of these confrontations are interesting in another respect. With the exception of *Python Crushing a Crocodile*, in which the snake bites the leg of the creature in a gesture similar to that in the *Laocoön*, the serpent attacks the throat of its victim. The reptile's jaw functions as a hand choking its prey or like the mouth of a predator cat in one of Barye's other groups. Other artists showed the boa crushing the crea-

ture, the serpent's mouth opened wide to swallow the animal whole.[33] In Barye's treatment, which does not conform to nature, Death clutches its victim by the throat.

Plasters of *Theseus Fighting the Centaur Biénor* (see fig. 47) and *Jaguar Devouring a Hare* (fig. 36) were submitted to the Salon of 1850–51. A bronze of the latter was commissioned by the State and exhibited at the Salon in 1852. *Jaguar Devouring a Hare* is thematically related to the animal confrontations of the 1830s. Like *Tiger Devouring a Gavial* and *Lion Crushing a Serpent*, this work was conceived and executed on a large scale. With these two submissions to the Salon, Barye made a case for monumental animal sculpture.[34]

The pose of the jaguar recurs in the small group *Jaguar Devouring a Crocodile* (fig. 37), undoubtedly from about the same time. A peculiar distortion in scale appears in both of these sculptures. In the smaller work, the jaguar physically dominates the crocodile. The protagonists in *Tiger Devouring a Gavial* are proportionate; the reptile in *Jaguar Devouring a Crocodile* is no match in size or strength for its feline enemy. With its head bent back and its mouth wide open in a cry of pain, the crocodile pathetically raises its right leg to fend off its assailant.

In *Jaguar Devouring a Hare*, on the other hand, the rabbit seems disproportionately large. Yet the piece is unusually affecting, not only because the victim is a gentle hare but also because of the subject's presentation. Called the tiger of the new world, the jaguar was considered as vicious and cruel as its counterpart, since it lived on prey and lost all courage once satiated.[35] *Jaguar Devouring a Hare* undoubtedly recalled to Bayre's contemporaries the story in which a lion, in a show of magnanimity, allows the rabbit it has in its grasp to live.[36] The tale was used to contrast the greatness of the

Fig. 35. *Python Crushing a Crocodile.*

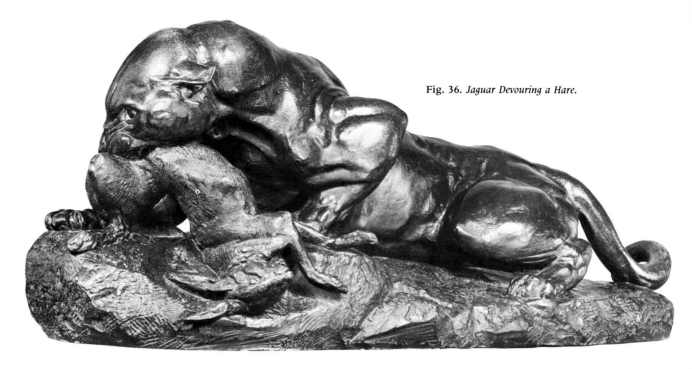

Fig. 36. *Jaguar Devouring a Hare.*

lion with the meanness of other cats. Here, the predator shows no mercy.

Through its formal elements, the work conveys the dramatic passion of this unequal encounter between powerful predator and feeble prey. With taut neck and tight leg muscles that push against the earth, the rapacious jaguar appears to be devouring the genitals of the victimized hare, whose limp body bends back in a deadly swoon. The image calls to mind Buffon's description of the tiger as an animal who "tears its prey for no other purpose than to plunge its head into the body."[37]

Of all Barye's confrontations, *Jaguar Devouring a Hare* is the most explicit in its allusion to sexual violation.[38] The gentleness of the hare is implied by the delicate softness of its fur so lovingly realized. In contrast, the jaguar's coat is slick. Its smooth, muscular body takes on a pronounced masculine sensuality; it appears sweaty from exertion.

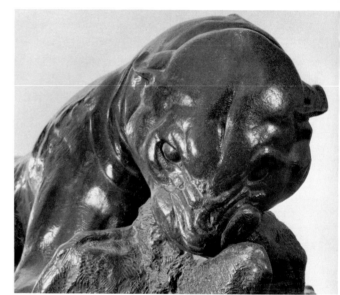

Fig. 38. Detail of *Jaguar Devouring a Hare.*

Fig. 37. *Jaguar Devouring a Crocodile.*

Ears bent back close to the neck, the jaguar's skull looms like a grotesque death's head over its victim (fig. 38). An obscene voluptuousness emanates from this drama of innocence ravished and destroyed. More than just another treatment of an animal confrontation, the image seems psychologically charged. Is it possible that the disturbing pathos of this group reflects Barye's own state of mind at the time? Delacroix recorded in his journal for March 10, 1847, the receipt of a letter announcing the funeral of Barye's daughter. The painter observed, "That unhappy man is going to be very sad and very lonely." The next day he attended the funeral and then commented on the absence of friends and the sculptor's reserve.[39] Was the creation of this sculpture thus prompted by an intense personal reaction to the death of a beloved child?

Barye's contemporaries, who responded to the work's sexual morbidity, recognized *Jaguar Devouring a Hare* as an extraordinary achievement. In his review of the Salon, Théophile Gautier commented on the voluptuousness of the jaguar and how it "revels in the orgasm of cruelty about to be enjoyed. . . ."[40] And Genevay, who judged the work to be Barye's *chef d'oeuvre*, added:

> See with what intoxication the brute drinks the blood; his veins seem gorged with pleasure, his lips quiver and his tail stiffens, his spine undulates, his sides palpitate, his ears flatten, his nostrils dilate, his very flesh creeps! Never was there a picture of the satiated cravings of the murderer rendered with such fearful intensity and by so energetic a hand.[41]

*Jaguar Devouring a Hare* remains one of the strongest and most intensely felt works in the artist's *oeuvre*.

Together, Barye's repertoire of animals, domestic and savage, is small. The species he depicted served as leitmotifs in his work, like the recurring characters in Balzac's *Human Comedy*. Whether treating lions, tigers, jaguars, panthers, crocodiles, dogs, bears, or deer, he showed them in different situations and moods—resting, vigilant, playful, fighting, struggling for existence. Barye presented his antagonists in moments of engagement and victory. Their violent confrontations take on the aura of natural dramas.

In the early nineteenth century, interest in human and comparative psychology was growing. It was felt that instinctual behavior in animals provided insight into human feelings.[42] The passionate pursuit of pleasure and the avoidance of pain were considered major drives in man as well as beast. Instant gratification with little thought of the future and no sense of moral responsibility was seen as an accepted way of life.[43] Barye's confrontations reflect these attitudes. In the life-and-death struggles he depicted, his protagonists became victims or voluptuaries. The intensity of the emotions displayed elicited strong associative reactions from the viewer. By visualizing an animal's inarticulate cries of pain or fear, by presenting a beast's instinctual need to destroy and violate, Barye's subjects, frought with intense terror or unrestrained passion, struck a sublime note in his audience.[44]

Fig. 39. Detail of "Rage" from Charles Bell, *Essays on the Anatomy of Expression in Painting.* Courtesy of Henry Francis du Pont Winterthur Museum Library: Collection of Printed Books and Periodicals.

Fig. 40. Detail of *Tiger Devouring a Gavial.* Louvre. Photograph: author.

Fig. 41. Detail of "The Contours of Eyes" from Johann Caspar Lavater, *Essays on Physiognomy*. Courtesy of Henry Francis du Pont Winterthur Museum Library: Collection of Printed Books and Periodicals. Taken from a page with eight pairs of eyes conveying different expressions: (7) represents the horror of rage and (8) a demoniac.

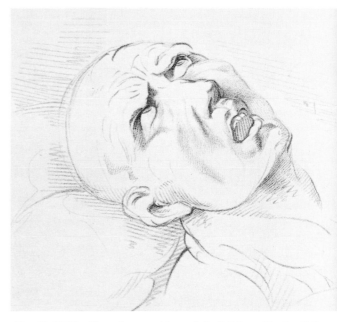

Fig. 42. "Of bodily pain, anguish, and death" from Charles Bell, *Essays on the Anatomy of Expression in Painting*. Courtesy of Henry Francis du Pont Winterthur Museum Library: Collection of Printed Books and Periodicals.

Fig. 43. Detail of *North African Horseman Surprised by a Serpent*.

Fig. 44. Detail of *Tiger Attacking a Stag*.

Representation of the passions was long considered central to an artist's concerns. In the seventeenth century, the French painter Charles Le Brun standardized for artists the ways in which to show various emotions.[45] Eventually, the study of expression became integral to academic training. In 1759, the Count of Caylus founded at the Ecole des Beaux-Arts a competition for the representation of human expression in sculpture and painting.[46] As a student at the Ecole, Barye was exposed to these ideas. He also had many opportunities to see diploma pieces by distinguished French sculptors such as Nicolas Sebastien Adam and Etienne Falconnet in which man's confrontation with a savage beast was the vehicle for exploring intense human feelings.[47] And famous works such as Puget's *Milo of Crotona* as well as copies after classical masterpieces, including the *Laocoön*, were accessible in the Tuileries and other public places.

Barye's *Milo of Crotona* (fig. 1) underscores the impact of these ideas on his development, as do mature works such as *Theseus Fighting the Minotaur* and *Theseus Fighting the Centaur Biénor* (see figs. 45, 47). His animal subjects, whether representations of beasts in moments of relaxation or in scenes of combat, are no less revealing, for in depicting the affection, fear, and rage of animals, the artist used emotion to define their natures. Early in his career, Barye was called "un savant physiologue," and another critic remarked that the sculptor was not content to deal with external forms but would rather explore the instinct, character, and temperament of his subjects by showing their attitudes and intimate passions.[48]

In his exploitation of emotions common to man and beast, Barye partook of the current interest in comparative psychology. As the contemporary British anatomist Charles Bell advised, "To learn the character of the human countenance when devoid of expression, and reduced to the state of brutality, we must have recourse to the lower animals; and as I have already hinted, study their expression, their timidity, their watchfulness, their state of excitement, and their ferociousness." Bell contended that instinctual feelings were common to all animals.[49]

Particularly telling for Barye are Bell's comments on carnivorous creatures. Rage in them was "distinguished by the most remarkable strength of expression. The eyeball is terrible, and the retraction of the flesh of the lips indicated the most savage fury. . . . The great animals of prey, the lion and the tiger, are quite incapable of any other expression or feature. . . ."[50] While there is no documentary evidence that Barye knew Bell's treatise, the correspondence between the anatomist's illustration of rage in man (fig. 39)[51] and the sculptor's depiction of the same emotion in animal (fig. 40) argues for Barye's early familiarity with Bell's well-known study.

Barye adapted conventional modes of expressing human emotions to his interpretation of animal passions. For example, the wrinkling of the nose and the furrowing of the brow in aroused beasts are in essence variations on portrayals of demonic rage (figs. 38, 41). The pain and fear expressed by the prey, whose open mouth seems to emit a silent cry, also had its human parallels (figs. 42-44).[52]

Writing a few years after Barye's death, Paul Souriau, stimulated by recent developments in photography, differentiated in *The Aesthetics of Movement* (1889) between the expression of motion and the impression of motion, between the emotion of the subject and the reaction of the viewer.[53] This distinction is critical in evaluating Barye's achievement. The sculptor manipulated forms to achieve effects; he used the emotions of his subjects to touch the emotions of his audience. As one early critic observed about *Tiger Devouring a Gavial*, "Life and suffering are expressed with such force and truth that the illusion is complete. One really suffers in looking at it. . . ."[54]

Captured in momentary instinctual activities, Barye's subjects are often portrayed with a wealth of detail that encourages the viewer to accept what is shown as true. His work is, as was claimed by his contemporaries, a marriage between science and art.[55] Yet in his animal dramas, passion, not anatomy, was his true subject. It could be said of Barye, as it was of his friend Delacroix, that he was "passionately in love with passion and coldly determined to seek ways to express passion by the most visible means."[56] In his intense depictions of life-and-death struggles, Barye found the way.

---

# NOTES

1   Honoré de Balzac, *Cousin Bette*, trans. Marion Ayton Crawford (1965; rpt. Harmondsworth, Middlesex, England, 1984), 218–19.

2   A. Genevay, "A. L. Barye, 1796–1875," in William Thompson Walters, comp., *Antoine-Louis Barye from the French of Various Critics* (Baltimore, 1885), 17. Genevay quotes "N.," *Le National*, April 21, 1833.

3   Théophile Silvestre, *Histoire des Artistes Vivants, Français et Etrangers* (Paris, 1857), 201.

4   Nancy Ann Finlay, *Animal Themes in the Painting of Eugène Delacroix* (Ann Arbor, MI, 1984), 72.

5   Barye also created over two hundred watercolors as well as oils in which animal combats figure prominently. For the watercolors, see Charles O. Zieseniss, *Les Aquarelles de Barye: Étude critiques et catalogue raisonné* (Paris, 1956). There is no study of his oils.

6   For a discussion of the first two categories, see in this catalogue Elizabeth Briggs Lynch, "Barye's Mythological Subjects," and Barbara

J. Stephanic, "Barye's Exotic Hunt Scenes."

7   Many of these measured drawings are at the Ecole Nationale Supérieure des Beaux-Arts, Paris; other examples are at the Baltimore Museum of Art and the Walters Art Gallery in Baltimore. Barye's mathematical approach to sculpture was apparently shared by his contemporary François Rude. See Charles Rosen and Henri Zerner, *Romanticism and Realism: The Mythology of Nineteenth-Century Art* (New York, 1984), 9, where they quote Jean-Baptiste Carpeaux's favorable remarks about Rude.

8   Alfonz Lengyel, *Life and Art of Antoine-Louis Barye* (Dubuque, IA, 1963), 5. Also see Eugène Guillaume, "Introduction," in Roger Ballu, *L'Oeuvre de Barye* (Paris, 1890), xxii–xxiii.

9   Louis Rousseau and Ceran Lemonnier, *Promenades au Jardin des Plantes* (Paris, 1837), talks about the library, when it was founded, and what it contained. In addition, the Duke of Orléans reportedly lent Barye a number of books; see Guillaume, "Introduction," in Ballu, *L'Oeuvre de Barye*, xxiii. "Registres d'entrée" of the menagerie, preserved at the Bibliothèque Centrale of the museum, reveal that specimens were occasionally donated by members of the Orléans family.

10   Arsène Alexandre, *Antoine-Louis Barye* (Paris, 1889), 43. Glenn F. Benge, *Antoine-Louis Barye: Sculptor of Romantic Realism* (University Park, PA, 1984), 9, comments on how Barye never allowed "mere factual data to outweigh the expressiveness of his artistic imagery." For a discussion of Barye's scientific approach to his subject, see Roger Henri Gorvel Thierry, *La Sculpture animalière de Barye vue par un Vétérinaire*, (doctorate thesis, Ecole Nationale Vétérinaire d'Alfort, 1982), 18–33.

11   Barye's use of the facial features of animals to comment on their natures parallels the then current artistic interest in human physiognomy to reveal character. The idea that physical appearance provides a clue to moral character is of ancient origin. A key eighteenth-century figure in the theory of human physiognomy was Johann Caspar Lavater, a Swiss theologian and writer, whose multi-volumed work on the subject (see n. 18 below) went through several editions in various languages. For recent studies dealing with Lavater's impact on art, see especially George Levitine, "The Influence of Lavater and Girodet's *Expression des Sentiments de l'Âme*," *Art Bulletin*, 37, no. 1 (March 1954), 33–34; and Eve Twose Kliman, "Delacroix's Lions and Tigers: A Link between Man and Nature," *Art Bulletin*, 64, no. 3 (September 1982), 448–450.

12   Benge, *Barye: Sculptor*, documents Barye's wide knowledge of the art of the past; see especially pp. 9, 115, 134, but also the comparisons he makes throughout. Numerous artists treated the lion and horse theme: Giambologna, Massimilano Soldani, Antonio Susini, Johann Elias Ridinger, and George Stubbs, to name just a few. The lion and bull, although not as common, was also attempted by Giambologna, Susini, and Soldani, among others.

13   Charles Blanc, "The Exhibition of Barye's Works at the Ecole des Beaux-Arts" in Walters, *Barye*, 54.

14   *Tiger Devouring a Gavial* and *Lion Crushing a Serpent* are reductions of the works exhibited, which are now in the Louvre. The reductions probably date from about the same period as the large pieces. The Corcoran's examples were undoubtedly cast much later.

15   Benge, *Barye: Sculptor*, 33–34.

16   Finlay, *Animal Themes*, 56, discusses the presence of live and stuffed tigers in Paris. For information on the arrival of animals to the Jardin des Plantes, see "Registre d'entrée," No. 25, Bibliothèque Centrale, Museum National d'Histoire Naturelle, Paris. The tiger was admitted on August 28, 1830, and died July 17, 1839.

17   Quoted in Walters, *Barye*, 16. Delécluze's comments were reproduced elsewhere; see Alexandre, *Barye*, 44.

18   Johann Caspar Lavater, *Essays on Physiognomy*, trans. Thomas Holcroft (3 vols; London, 1804), II, 171–72, 175, 179; also George Louis Leclerc, Count de Buffon, *Natural History: General and Particular*, trans. William Smellie (20 vols.; London, 1812), VI, 275–76. An 1827 guide of the menagerie at the Jardin des Plantes echoes these sentiments at a time when Barye was studying there; quoted in Finlay, *Animal Themes*, 50.

19   Benge, *Barye: Sculptor*, 25, mentions the recurring "motif of the predator's mouth clamped into the flesh of its prey." He also describes how the predators embrace their prey; p. 110.

20 Gustave Planche's negative comments on Barye's excessive detail have been frequently reprinted. See, for example, Charles DeKay, *Barye: Life and Works of Antoine-Louis Barye, Sculptor* (1889; rpt. New York, 1974), 35; and in Benge, *Barye: Sculptor*, 32. Also see Ballu, *L'Oeuvre de Barye*, 34, for negative comments by others.

21 Ballu, *L'Oeuvre de Barye*, 35.

22 Jacques de Caso, "The Origin of Barye's *Ape Riding a Gnu*," *Journal of the Walters Art Gallery*, 27–28 (1964–1965), 69, identifies the source of Barye's sculpture as Thomas Landseer's illustration from John Henry Barrow, *Characteristic Sketches of Animals* (1832). Lee Johnson, "Delacroix, Barye and 'The Tower Menagerie': An English Influence on French Romantic Animal Pictures," *Burlington Magazine*, 106, no. 738 (September 1964), 419, points to an illustration by William Harvey in his 1829 book on the London Tower menagerie as the source for Barye's watercolor *Python Attacking a Leopard*. Thomas Bewick in *A General History of Quadrupeds* (Newcastle upon Tyne, 1807), 221, mentions that tigers eat alligators and crocodiles.

23 For a political interpretation of this work, see Benge, *Barye: Sculptor*, 31, 35.

24 Another composition by Northcote, *Vulture and Lamb*, is similar to Barye's *Eagle Holding a Heron*, but other prototypes for Barye's treatment of this subject can be found. All three prints by Northcote are in the collection of the Yale Center for British Art, New Haven, Connecticut.

25 The view of the snake as the embodiment of evil has its roots, of course, in the Judeo-Christian religion. This view was also expressed in contemporary natural histories and in works such as Lavater, *Physiognomy*, II, 191.

26 Among writers expressing this point of view were: Buffon, *Natural History*, VI, 191–92; George Cuvier, *Tableau élémentaire de l'histoire naturelle* (Paris, 1798), 117, and in *Le Règne animals* (Paris, 1817), I, 160; Lavater, *Physiognomy*, II, 169, 173. Frédéric Cuvier, *Dictionnaire des science naturelles* (Strasbourg, 1817), VIII, 211, 215, disagreed and took issue with Buffon.

27 Eve Twose Kliman, "Delacroix's Lions and Tigers: A Link Between Man and Nature," *Art Bulletin*, 64, no. 3 (September 1982), 447. This kind of animal imagery occurs frequently in Balzac's *Human Comedy*; see, for example, *Cousin Bette*, 82, 111, 190, 372.

28 Barye rarely depicted the lioness, which writers described as weak, insidious, and cruel. See Lavater, *Physiognomy*, II, 173. Two exceptions in bronze are *Lioness of Senegal* and *Lioness of Algeria*; there are also a few watercolors.

29 Illustrated in Stuart Pivar, *The Barye Bronzes: A Catalogue Raisonné* (Woodbridge, Suffolk, 1974), A196, 236. An example of this work was once part of the Corcoran's collection.

30 For examples, see Zieseniss, *Les Aquarelles*, F8-F11. A37 and A39 are watercolors depicting a confrontation between a lion and a python. There are also a number of watercolors dealing only with pythons as well as numerous drawings. Johnson, "Delacroix," 419, dates *Python Attacking a Leopard* around 1830, but the work could be later.

31 There is a question as to the exact date of founding of the Reptile House. *Guide des Étrangers dans le Museum d'Histoire Naturelle* (Paris, 1855), 60–61, gives 1836 as the date; Paul Antoine Cap, *Le Museum d'Histoire Naturelle* (Paris, 1854), 170, says 1839; and Finlay, *Animal Themes*, 65, puts it in 1837.

32 *Nouveau Dictionnaire d'Histoire Naturelle Appliquée aux Arts* (Paris, 1816), III, 510–11. Benge, *Barye: Sculptor*, 98–99, discusses *North African Horseman Surprised by a Serpent*. For additional remarks, see also Stephanic, "Barye's Exotic Hunt Scenes" in this catalogue. There are several examples of confrontations between animals, including men, and serpents in English art. Benge mentions Henry Fuseli (*Barye: Sculptor*, 99). James Ward treated serpent confrontations on several occasions; one of his compositions, *Liboya Seizing a Tyger*, was illustrated in *The Port Folio* in September, 1810.

33 See, for example, the compositions by Fuseli and Ward noted above.

34 Benge, *Barye: Sculptor*, 48.

35 Buffon, *Natural History*, VI, 312.

36 Finlay, *Animal Themes*, 58.

37 Buffon, *Natural History*, VI, 276.

38 Benge, *Barye: Sculptor*, 110, in discussing *Tiger Overturning an Antelope*, refers to the sexual way in which "the tiger's tail brushes the antelope's genitalia." For an illustration of this work, see Pivar, *Barye Bronzes*, A66, 145.

39 Eugène Delacroix, *The Journal of Eugène Delacroix*, ed. Hubert Wellington, trans. Lucy Norton (1951; rpt. Oxford, 1980), 71.

40 Quoted in Benge, *Barye: Sculptor*, 47.

41 Quoted in Walters, *Barye*, 25. For other praise of this work, see Ballu, *L'Oeuvre de Barye*, 105; and Guillaume, "Introduction," in Ballu, *L'Oeuvre de Barye*, xxvii.

42 See, for example, Charles Bell, *Essays on the Anatomy of Expression in Painting* (London, 1806), 85, quoted below. For general studies on the development of psychiatry in the early nineteenth century, see Mark D. Altschule, *Roots of Modern Psychiatry* (New York and London, 1957), particularly the section dealing with Broussais' theories, 62–64. Also see Franz G. Alexander and Sheldon T. Selesnick, *The History of Psychiatry* (New York, 1966) especially 141–42.

43 Honoré de Balzac, *Lost Illusions*, trans. Herbert J. Hunt (Harmondsworth, Middlesex, England, 1986), 409. In *Lost Illusions*, Balzac talks about young people, *viveurs*, who live for the moment, but such figures are frequently encountered in his novels and presumably reflect existing attitudes.

44 See Eugène Véron, "Exposition of Barye's Works at the Palace of the Beaux-Arts," in Walters, *Barye*, 33. The pleasure-pain principle, particularly as it relates to self-preservation, are central to Edmund Burke's *A Philosophical Enquiry into the Origin of Our Ideas of the Sublime and Beautiful* (1757; rpt. Notre Dame, IN, 1968), ed. J. T. Boulton, especially pt. I, sections II and VI. Burke discusses at some length powerful forces in nature such as wild animals with their inarticulate cries capable of arousing sublime and fearful sensations in man (pt. II, sections II and XX). Burke's influence in France has been well documented; see Boulton's introduction, cxx–cxxii.

45 First published in 1698, *Méthode pour apprendre à dessiner les passions* went through many editions and translations. Although Le Brun's examples were challenged, the ideas recur throughout the eighteenth and early nineteenth centuries in the writings of Lavater (see n. 18 above) and others. For a discussion of artistic expression, see Brewster Rogerson, "The Art of Painting the Passions," *Journal of the History of Ideas*, 14 (1953), 68–94. Frederic Cummings, in "Charles Bell and *The Anatomy of Expression*," *Art Bulletin*, 46, no. 2 (June 1964), 191–203, reviews the literature. Glenn F. Benge, in *The Sculpture of Antoine-Louis Barye in American Collections* (Ann Arbor, MI, 1969), discusses Emeric-David's influential *Recherches sur l'art statuaire* (1801), particularly as it relates to the representation of the passions, pp. 107–109.

46 For a discussion of this competition at the Ecole des Beaux-Arts, see Antoinette Le Normand Romain, "Concours de la tête d'expression," in *La Sculpture Française au XIXᵉ Siècle* (Paris, 1986), 42–48.

47 Adam's *Prometheus* and Falconet's *Milo of Crotona* are in the Louvre, along with other diploma pieces.

48 G. Laviron and B. Galbacio in their review of the 1833 Salon called Barye "un savant physiologue"; quoted in Lengyel, *Life and Art*, 16. Ballu, *L'Oeuvre de Barye*, 78.

49 Charles Bell, *Essays on the Anatomy of Expression in Painting* (London, 1806), 85.

50 *Ibid.*, 86.

51 *Ibid.*, 139, for a description of rage.

52 Precedent for this motif extends back to the *Laocoön*; however, in French art of the seventeenth and eighteenth centuries can be found many examples, notably in Puget's and in Falconet's *Milo of Crotona* and in Adam's *Prometheus*; see n. 47 above.

53 Paul Souriau, *The Aesthetics of Movement*, trans. and ed. Manon Souriau (Amherst, MA, 1983), 81, 83.

54 "A.," "Beaux-Arts. Salon de 1831. Sculpture." *L'Artiste*, 1, no. 18 (1831), 221.

55 Guillaume, "Introduction," in Ballu, *L'Oeuvre de Barye*, xxxi–xxxii.

56 Charles Baudelaire, *Curiosités esthétiques* (Paris, 1962), 426. Silvestre, *Histoire*, 201, notes that Barye was "au fond extrement passionné."

# V

# Barye's

# MYTHOLOGICAL SUBJECTS

Elizabeth Briggs Lynch

Beyond the modern perception of Barye as the Romantic *animalier sans parallèle*, another dimension of the sculptor's *oeuvre* is worthy of note. In addition to animal pieces, Barye executed a number of works in which humans are present, including a significant group with mythological subjects or motifs. Those in the Corcoran's collection are *Theseus Fighting the Minotaur* (fig. 45), *Theseus Fighting the Centaur Biénor* (fig. 47), *Lapith (Theseus) Fighting a Centaur* (fig. 48), *Roger and Angelica on the Hippogriff* (fig. 50), *Minerva* (fig. 52), and *Juno* (fig. 53).

Works derived from mythological themes recur throughout Barye's *oeuvre*, and he executed several such pieces as a student at the Ecole des Beaux-Arts. In 1819, the subject of Milo of Crotona (fig. 1) was assigned by the jury of the Prix de Rome competition in the medal section of the Ecole. Barye's entry won an honorable mention. For another competition at the Ecole in 1823, he presented *Hector Reproaching Paris*, a relief that received first prize in the *esquisse* division.[1] Periodically throughout his life, Barye returned to similar topics. When depicting classical subjects, however, he often chose those in which animals play important roles. Of twelve works with mythological themes, only four offer the human figure without an accompanying animal.[2]

Twice Barye treated the story of Theseus, the legendary hero of Attica and the son of Aegeus, ruler of Athens. Barye chose to portray perhaps the best known episode from Theseus' life—his confrontation with the Minotaur—as well as one less familiar, the battle with the centaur Biénor. He may have been attracted to these

two events, both of which were taken from Ovid's *Metamorphoses*, because they included monstrous creatures. Perhaps the sculptor felt challenged by the problem implicit in creating a half-man, half-beast figure. Through these groups Barye was able to demonstrate his mastery of human and animal anatomy as he dealt with a mythological theme that, in the official hierarchy of categories of subjects, was considered significant.

Barye's interest in the Theseus legend may also have been due to his concurrent interest in certain animal subjects. *Theseus Fighting the Minotaur* was submitted to the Salon in 1843 along with two studies of bulls.[3] All three were rejected. In 1846, Barye had the Theseus group cast in bronze; a version was accepted for the Salon of 1851. Four years later, when the work was shown at the Universal Exposition of 1855, Achille Devéria called it "a small masterpiece in the antique style."[4]

*Theseus Fighting the Minotaur* represents the moment in the story when the hero struggles with the Minotaur, the fearsome offspring of Pasiphae and a bull. After killing the Minotaur, Theseus escapes from the labyrinth of King Minos with the help of Minos' daughter, Ariadne.[5] In Barye's version, however, the hero's physique does not reflect the ideal proportions of classical Greek sculptures of the fourth century B.C., which were then so admired. Rather, the form of Theseus, particularly the rendering of his hair, has been compared to the Archaic sculpture *Apollo Piombino*,[6] while his rigid pose and stocky proportions are reminiscent of figures on sixth-century B.C. vase painting.[7] Although the face and body of Theseus recall Archaic Greek figures, the treatment of

Fig. 45. *Theseus Fighting the Minotaur.*

the Minotaur seems very naturalistic. Its head bears a strong resemblance to Barye's sculptures of bulls. It has been suggested that for the intertwined pose of the two figures, Barye was influenced by a drawing of grappling boxers by Théodore Géricault.[8]

The subject of Theseus and the Minotaur had been treated frequently in sculpture in the late eighteenth and early nineteenth centuries.[9] Among sculptural treatments of the theme are the famous work by Antonio Canova (1782) and the piece by Etienne-Jules Ramey (1827) that had been in the Tuileries Gardens since 1832. Barye's contemporaries compared his version to that by Ramey (fig. 46), which was strongly influenced by Canova's composition.[10] Even though the two earlier works conformed to the accepted Neoclassical canon of ideal beauty (which Canova established in part), Barye used an Archaic stylistic model. Furthermore, Barye was likely aware of the versions by Canova and Ramey, but there is no evidence that he relied on them as sources. Indeed, Barye chose to show Theseus wielding a sword rather than the club favored by both of his predecessors. In this detail, Barye's interpretation of the myth may have been influenced by vase painting. While Ovid's account does not mention a specific weapon, a significant number of antique vases adorned with scenes of Theseus and the Minotaur show him with a sword.[11]

From 1805 to 1819, Canova also undertook the subject of Theseus' battle with a centaur. It is possible that Barye's choice of subject was prompted by, if not actually conceived in competition with, the work of that great Italian Neoclassicist. Yet Barye was unique in choosing the specific confrontation between Theseus and Biénor. Most artists, including Canova, depicted the

Fig. 48. *Lapith (Theseus) Fighting a Centaur.*

Fig. 47. *Theseus Fighting the Centaur Biénor.*

Fig. 46. Etienne-Jules Ramey, *Theseus and the Minotaur.* Marble. Tuileries.

Fig. 49. Antoine-Louis Barye, *Riders from the Parthenon Frieze.* Pencil drawing. Walters Art Gallery, Baltimore.

more generic subject of Theseus and a centaur. For his source, Barye turned to Ovid, who among ancient writers was the only one to identify the centaur as Biénor in his description of the battle of the Lapiths and centaurs. In his version of *Theseus Fighting the Centaur Biénor,* Barye adhered closely to Ovid's account of the episode, as related in Book XII of *Metamorphoses.* During the wedding of Perithous and Hippodamia, a Lapith princess, a centaur attempts to abduct the bride. Theseus and the other guests exact swift retribution on the centaurs. Ovid describes Theseus leaping upon Biénor's back, pulling his hair, and hitting him repeatedly about the head with a ''club of harden'd oak.''[12]

Barye conceived of the first version of *Lapith (Theseus) Fighting a Centaur* even before he began work on *Theseus Fighting the Minotaur.* This *esquisse* (fig. 48) has been dated ca. 1840.[13] According to Arsène Alexandre, Barye kept this work in his studio over a number of years and re-worked it again and again.[14] He arrived at the final version (fig. 47) under the impetus of a commission he received from the State in January 1849, undoubtedly a determining factor in the artist's decision to increase its scale. The work, exhibited at the Salon of 1850, was listed in the catalogue as *Un Centaure et un Lapithe, groupe plâtre.* In 1855, it was given in Barye's sales catalogue as *Thésée combattant le centaure Biénor.* Why Barye changed the title between 1850 and 1855 is not known, but he may have wished to differentiate between the earlier *esquisse* and the more refined finished version.

In addition to enlarging the work, Barye made a number of substantive changes in the final version, the most notable being alterations in the base. He added a mass of vegetation directly under the centaur's belly, which serves to direct the eye upward. The centaur's bent foreleg and his tail were made to curve toward the central mass, and the awkward angle of the Lapith's back was lessened. Together, the higher base and changes in pose contributed to an impression of greater stability and balance. Barye also subtly altered the facial features and proportions of the two figures. In the final version, details of the centaur's hair, beard, and face, so reminiscent of Hellenistic sculpture, appear more naturalistic than in the earlier work. The later conception of Theseus not only reflects a classical composure but also is more generalized and ideal.

This large version proved popular among critics, including Théophile Gautier, who wrote in 1866:

The *Centaur Overcome by a Lapith* [sic] shows that this Romantic, proscribed by juries, was the modern master of statuary who most closely approached Phidias and Greek sculpture. This Lapith, with his robust and simple forms, beautiful as the ideal, true as nature, could have figured on the front of the Parthenon, by the side of the Ilyssus, and the centaur could have mingled with the cavalcade of the metopes.[15]

Gautier correctly linked *Theseus Fighting the Centaur Biénor* to the Parthenon sculpture, for the subject of the combat between the Lapiths and the centaurs is indeed treated on the metopes. Theseus' pose, specifically his raised arm and the exaggerated curve of his back, incorporates a motif from the Parthenon's *Cavalcade of Riders* frieze, which Barye copied (fig. 49).[16] He could well have had this group in mind when he composed his own work. Similarly, Barye may have based Theseus' proportions on those of the *Diskobolos.* Eugène Guillaume, who acquired many of the sculptor's drawings after his death, studied Barye's drawings and measurements of the *Diskobolos* and noted similarities between the proportions of the two.[17]

To heighten the emotional tension of the work, Barye contrasted the calm, controlled composure of Theseus with the extreme agitation of the centaur. Intensifying the violent action, the centaur twists and struggles, his face distorted by anguish and passion. Given the final group, it seems likely that Barye intended to compare the rational, human quality of Theseus with the irrational, bestial character of the centaur.

The juxtaposition of a rational, thinking being with an emotional, irrational one provides visual expression of the concept of the great Chain of Being, an idea popular in the eighteenth and early nineteenth centuries which held that all living things could be arranged from the lowest to the highest level of being, with man as the link between earthly and heavenly creatures.[18] This concept had classical roots in the *Republic* and *Timaeus* of Plato, in which man represented the highest and morally best level of a hierarchy of beings. In keeping with the nineteenth-century interpretation of this idea, both *Theseus Fighting the Centaur Biénor* and *Theseus Fighting the Minotaur* would have been understood to embody the triumph of logic and reason over unthinking, brute strength

Although not a classical subject, *Roger and Angelica on the Hippogriff* can be considered in the context of the Theseus theme. As with the Minotaur and the centaur, Barye was probably attracted to the subject of the hippogriff, a fantastical hybrid animal, because of the challenge it presented.

Most sources agree that in 1840, the Duke of Montpensier, one of the five sons of Louis-Philippe, commissioned Barye to create a *garniture de cheminée* consisting of one central group and a pair of candelabra.[19] Given the romantic subject matter, however, it is conceivable that the ensemble was not commissioned until 1846, on the occasion of the duke's marriage to the sister of the queen of Spain. Undoubtedly the duke was impressed by Barye's work on the *surtout de table* for his brother, the Duke of Orléans. It has been suggested that Barye selected the subject,[20] an episode from Ariosto's *Orlando Furioso*. The choice, however, may have been dictated by Louis-Philippe's connection to the House of Este, of which Roger was the legendary progenitor. Furthermore, Ariosto first published the poem in 1516, under the patronage of Cardinal Ippolito d'Este. Louis-Philippe's mother was the daughter of Marie-Thérèse Felicité d'Este-Modena.

Set in the Carolingian era, *Orlando Furioso* consists of a series of chivalric romances. A substantial portion of the poem involves the hapless pursuit of the beautiful Angelica, princess of Cathay, by various suitors. Among them is Roger the Paladin. The particular episode Barye depicted is taken from Canto X, in which Roger, flying by on his hippogriff (a mythological beast of half-horse, half-eagle), sees the lovely princess chained to a rock on the Isle of Tears. After he rescues her from the sea monster Orc, they flee together on the hippogriff.

Even though *Orlando Furioso* was a popular literary source for Romantic artists, sculptural precedents for this specific subject did not exist in the nineteenth century. Ingres had painted Roger and Angelica two times, once in 1819 and again in 1839. (These works are respectively now in the Louvre and the National Gallery, London.) Given the episode's similarities to the myth of Perseus and Andromeda, it is not surprising that nineteenth-century painters, including Ingres, typically employed the iconographic formula of the better known story. Apparently Barye turned to other sources for his composition. A minor Romantic artist, Louis Rioult, painted in 1824 Roger and Angelica embracing on the back of the flying hippogriff (now in the

**Fig. 50.** *Roger and Angelica on the Hippogriff.*

Louvre). His version, however, is static and two-dimensional in appearance.

It is more likely that Barye was influenced by the illustrations that accompanied a French translation of *Orlando Furioso* published in 1839.[21] Barye's grouping relates to the pose of the figures in the illustration *Roger et Angélique sur l'Hippogriffe* (fig. 51). While the demeanor of those figures is relatively demure, Barye invested his work with an element of eroticism, which is also present in the prose text. The 1839 translation describes the paladin often turning around to his pretty companion to press kisses upon her throat. Roger changes his course and lands at a secluded spot so he might seduce Angelica. He is frustrated by his armor, but by the time he divests himself of it, the princess has employed a magic ring to disappear.[22] Barye captured the flavor of the episode in his composition. Roger gazes ardently at Angelica, who modestly averts her head and seems to hold herself aloof from his embrace. The movement inherent in the coiled tail of the dolphin below and the headlong flight of the hippogriff add an element of excitement and urgency to the scene. Quite similarly, the image of a galloping horse was recognized in nineteenth-century France as a symbol of unbridled passion.[23]

This group is unlike any other in Barye's *oeuvre*, not

Fig. 52. *Minerva.*

Fig. 53. *Juno.*

Fig. 51. A. Jourdain, ''Roger et Angélique sur l'Hippogriffe'' from Ludovico Ariosto, *Roland furieux.* Library of Congress.

only in terms of the subject matter but also in its erotic quality. Although the work is relatively large, it has a jewellike, decorative quality about it, which recalls Barye's tenure with the goldsmith Fauconnier. Significantly, this piece, which was ultimately flanked by an elaborate pair of candelabra, may have been intended to adorn the top of a clock.[24] The fact that the sculpture was initially designed for the private delectation of his young patron, perhaps on the occasion of his marriage to a princess, undoubtedly affected Barye's approach to the subject.

Barye designed the *Nine Light Candelabra* (fig. 65) to complement *Roger and Angelica on the Hippogriff*. Its decorative, embellished style harmonizes with the delicate silhouette of the central piece. In its entirety the candelabrum includes nine figures: the goddesses Juno, Minerva, and Venus seated at the base; three chimeras on the middle level; and above the nine branches, the Three Graces. (The top element is missing from the Corcoran's pair.) In his first sales catalogue of 1847, Barye offered separately-cast editions of two of the goddesses, Minerva and Juno (figs. 52, 53). The third goddess, Venus, was not offered singly for sale until 1855, when the slightly altered figure was listed in the sales catalogue as *une Néreide*. This work may provide the key to Barye's source of inspiration for the female forms in the *garniture de cheminée*, for it corresponds closely to the nereids that appear on the sixteenth-century Fontaine des Innocents by Jean Goujon in Paris. Thus Barye maintained a degree of homogeneity throughout the ensemble by employing a particular female type based on Goujon's model.

Even if Barye depended on earlier sculptural sources for his rendering of human forms, he let his imagination soar when he produced the strange hybrid forms of the Minotaur, the centaur, and the hippogriff. These creatures might be viewed as the perfect embodiment of Barye's Romantic naturalism. Through them, he struck harmonious balance between minute attention to anatomical realism and the freedom of artistic creativity.

## NOTES

1 The relief is in the collection of the Ecole Nationale Supérieure des Beaux-Arts.

2 The twelve works are: *Milo of Crotona*, two versions of *Hercules Bearing the Erymanthean Boar*, *Hector Reproaching Paris*, *Theseus Fighting the Minotaur*, *Theseus Fighting a Centaur*, *Theseus Fighting the Centaur Biénor*, *Apollo Guiding the Sun Chariot*, two *River Gods*, *Leda and the Swan*, and *Apollo*. Not included are *Minerva*, *Juno*, and *Venus*, originally conceived as part of the *Nine Light Candelabra*.

3 According to the Louvre Archives for 1843, all four of the animal sculptures that Barye submitted that year, two of bulls and two of snakes, were "studies" in bronze. See *La Sculpture Française au XIXᵉ Siècle* (Paris, 1986), 419, X, n. 6.

4 Quoted in Charles Saunier, *Barye* (Paris, 1925), 45.

5 Probably the best known account of the exploits of Theseus is to be found in Book VIII of Ovid's *Metamorphoses*, the literary source for Barye's other Theseus subject. For information on early sources for the Theseus myth, see Wilmon Brewer, *Ovid's Metamorphoses in European Culture*, vol. II (Boston, 1941).

6 It is worth noting that the *Apollo Piombino* entered the Louvre in 1834. Glenn F. Benge, *Antoine-Louis Barye: Sculptor of Romantic Realism* (University Park, PA, 1984), 8.

7 There is evidence of Barye's use of vase painting as a stylistic source, if not for this particular work; see Glenn F. Benge, "Barye, Flaxman and Phidias," *Acts of the 24th International Congress of the History of Art*, 6 (Bologna, 1982), 106 and 109–10, n. 39.

8 Barye's copy of Géricault's drawing is in the Walters collection (Inv. no. 37.2060). Benge also points out the resemblance of Barye's *Theseus Fighting the Minotaur* to antique representations of Herakles and Anteus. See Benge, "Barye's Use of Some Géricault Drawings," *Journal of the Walters Art Gallery*, 31–32 (1968–1969), 24.

9 H. W. Janson's index to Stanislas Lami's *Dictionnaire des Sculpteurs de l'École Française* lists ten different nineteenth-century French sculptural versions of Theseus and the Minotaur, excluding Barye's.

10 Roger Ballu, *L'Oeuvre de Barye* (Paris, 1890), xii.

11 Examples of vases showing Theseus with a sword are the red figure kylix signed by the painter Epiketos, from Vulci, in the British Museum of Art and the red figure kylix signed by the Chachrylion Potter in Antichita d'Etruria, Florence.

12 Publius Ovidius Naso, *Ovid's Metamorphoses*, Book XII (New York, 1961), 402.

13 Benge, *Barye: Sculptor*, 48.

14 Arsène Alexandre, *Antoine-Louis Barye* (Paris, 1889), 30.

15 Quoted in Ballu, *L'Oeuvre de Barye*, 105.

16 Glenn F. Benge, "Napoleon I Crowned by History and the Fine Arts: The Drawings for Barye's Apotheosis Pediment for the New Louvre," *Art Journal*, 38, no. 3 (Spring 1979), 166, 170, n. 13. According to Benge, Barye would have been familiar with the Parthenon scenes through illustrations in the French translation of James Stuart and Nicholas Revett *The Antiquities of Athens*, which was published in Paris in 1835.

17 Eugène Guillaume, "Introduction," in Ballu, *L'Oeuvre de Barye*, xxvii.

18 In the late eighteenth and early nineteenth centuries, the scientific applications of the Chain of Being principle were explored by such great naturalists as Cuvier and Lamarck. Barye was very familiar with the theories of Cuvier and Lamarck, authors of two of the most widely read treatises on zoology of the early nineteenth century. For further discussion of the concept of the Chain of Being, see Arthur O. Lovejoy, *The Great Chain of Being* (Cambridge, MA, 1936).

19 The date given in early catalogues of the Corcoran's collection is 1846.

20 See Ballu, *L'Oeuvre de Barye*, 79; Saunier, *Barye*, 29; and Stuart Pivar, *The Barye Bronzes: A Catalogue Raisonné* (Woodbridge, Suffolk, 1974), 7.

21 Ludovico Ariosto, *Roland furieux*, trans. M. A. Mazuy (Paris, 1839).

22 *Ibid.*, 232.

23 See, for example, Léon Cogniet's *Rape of Rebecca* (1828, Wallace Collection, London) and Ary Scheffer's *The Dead Move Fast* (1830, Musée des Beaux-Arts, Lille). Nancy Ann Finlay, *Animal Themes in the Painting of Eugène Delacroix* (Ann Arbor, MI, 1984), 30.

24 Lami, *Dictionnaire des Sculpteurs*, 76, and Ballu, *L'Oeuvre de Barye*, 79, both mention that the piece was intended to be placed on top of a clock.

Fig. 54. *Charles VI Surprised in the Forest of Mans.* Louvre. Photograph: Musées Nationaux.

# VI

# Barye's

## HISTORICAL GENRE
## AND THE HOUSE OF ORLEANS

Edward J. Nygren

Excluding hunting scenes and classical subjects, there are only fourteen historical figurative bronzes in Barye's oeuvre, virtually all of which are equestrians. With few exceptions, most were created from about 1833 to 1840.[1] The Corcoran presently owns eight of these works; a ninth piece, *Gaston de Foix*, was once part of the collection.

It is the premise of this essay that six of these historical figurative sculptures from the 1830s and early 1840s deal, directly or indirectly, with Orléanist themes. An exception is the exotic *Tartar Warrior Checking His Horse* (see fig. 86). While a few are known to have been commissioned by members of Louis-Philippe's family, others may well have been encouraged by royal patronage. During this period, Barye's professional relationship with the king's family was close. In 1833, the sculptor exhibited a bust of the Duke of Orléans (present whereabouts unknown) as well as the group *Charles VI Surprised in the Forest of Mans* (fig. 54), which he created for the duke's sister Marie. Also in that year, the State bought *Lion Crushing a Serpent*. About the same time, the Duke of Orléans ordered a *surtout de table*, the most important and largest private commission Barye received from the family. This was followed a few years later by the creation of candelabra and *Roger and Angelica on the Hippogriff* for the Duke of Montpensier.[2]

The degree to which Barye embraced the political principles of Louis-Philippe's regime cannot be documented; however, the figurative bronzes he produced for or about the house of Orléans provide an intriguing body of work worthy of speculation. Several of the

pieces for the *surtout*, such as *Lion Hunt* and *Tiger Hunt* (figs. 22, 24), as well as the derivative compositions *Two Arab Horsemen Killing a Lion* and *Indian Mounted on an Elephant Crushing a Tiger* (figs. 23, 21), may be allusions to Louis-Philippe's imperial ambitions in North Africa and Asia, respectively. At the time that Barye was working on the *surtout* for the Duke of Orléans, his patron was actively engaged in France's conquest of Algeria. Other works in the series, for example, *Bear Hunt* and *Bull Hunt* (figs. 55, 56), seem to refer to glorious periods in French history of particular interest to the Orléanists. The costumes in *Bear Hunt* suggest a scene set in the time of Francis I, who, like Louis-Philippe, had succeeded his cousin. Moreover, under Louis-Philippe, Fontainebleau, the chateau of Francis I in the Loire valley, was restored and became "a symbol of the continuity of the French dynasty."[3] Two individual works—*Peasant of the Middle Ages* (fig. 57) and *A Cavalier*—are derived from this group.[4] *Bull Hunt*, with its horsemen dressed in fifteenth-century armor, could well allude to the time when Joan of Arc, Maid of Orléans, helped Charles VII unify France.

Despite the fact that bear and bull hunts no longer occurred in France, and tiger and lion hunts were pursuits in exotic lands, Barye's hunting scenes and their derivations underscore the importance of the sport in the education of a nobleman. The young duke, who had served in Belgium in the early 1830s and was in Algeria at the end of the decade, had reportedly lent the sculptor a "great number of books on hunting, combat and travel," where the connection between the hunt

Fig. 55. *Bear Hunt*. Walters Art Gallery, Baltimore.

and warfare would have been expressed or implied.[5] Such books frequently contained illustrations in which class distinctions were clearly delineated and the valor of the nobility emphasized. These ideas were also easily accessible in current popular works well known to Barye, such as Count Buffon's *Natural History*. When discussing stag hunting, for example, Buffon differentiated between "the nobles, whose business is arms and hunting; and the vulgar, who are occupied in cultivating the earth." He went on to say:

> In polished societies . . . to ennoble this most beneficial and respectable of all exercises, it [hunting] has been formed into an art. The chase of the stag requires a species of

knowledge, which can only be learned by experience: it implies a royal assemblage of men, horses, and dogs, all so trained, practised, and disciplined, that their movements, their researchers, and their skill, must concur in producing one common end.[6]

At the same time that Barye created the *surtout*, he also designed a series of equestrian sculptures that refer to the house of Orléans. It is, I believe, in these consciously historical figures that the propagandistic intentions of the artist or of his royal patrons are most evident. The subjects themselves are revealing. As equestrian images, they provide visual associations with the long tradition of military and imperial portraiture that extends back to classical times. Barye would have known such modern examples of the genre as *Louis XIV* (1836) by Cartellier and Petitot at Versailles and *Henry IV* (1816) by Lemot in Paris.[7] Yet *General Bonaparte* (fig. 58), *Charles VII Victorious* (fig. 59), *Duke of Orléans* (fig. 61), *Equestrienne in 1830 Dress* (fig. 62), or *Gaston de Foix* (fig. 60) are more than just variations on an established tradition with a prescribed and conventional format. In my opinion, they, along with *Charles VI Surprised in the Forest of Mans* (fig. 54), either depict personages directly related to the Orléanist name or reflect a political position of the regime. By examining these figures in some detail, the nature of the ideas incorporated into them can be hypothesized.

Of these works, only *General Bonaparte*, executed in 1838, deals with a person who had no familial connection to the house of Orléans. The historical connection between Napoleon and Louis-Philippe, however, was substantial. They were, after all, contemporaries, and it could be argued that Louis-Philippe's ascension to the throne would not have occurred without the Napoleonic era. Equally important is the fact that Bonapartism was a critical issue for the new king, who wished to align himself with the revolutionary sentiments of

Fig. 56. *Bull Hunt*. Walters Art Gallery, Baltimore.

1789 and the nationalistic fervor of Napoleon rather than with the reactionary government of the restored monarchy of his cousins, Louis XVIII and Charles X.[8] Under the Citizen King, the tricolor once more became the flag of France, and the trappings of Bourbon absolutism were eschewed.

With the reestablishment of the Bourbon dynasty following the fall of Napoleon in 1814, those who had once supported the emperor became suspect while they remained a force in French politics. The death of the exiled Napoleon in 1821 and the repressive reign of Charles X made Bonapartism and the remembrance of lost freedoms and past imperial glories factors in the Revolution of 1830.

Louis-Philippe sought to exploit the Napoleonic legend without putting his own regime in jeopardy. To this end, he resisted pressure to bring the remains of Napoleon back to France at the same time that he commissioned elaborate compositions honoring Napoleon's victories for the Salle of 1830 at Versailles.[9] In 1840, Louis-Philippe's son, the Duke of Joinville, accompanied the body of the former emperor from Saint Helena to Paris, where it was interred in the Hôtel des Invalides. By that time the Citizen King had lost most of his popular support and was seeking ways in which to ingratiate his autocratic government with the people.

Barye's *General Bonaparte* is in keeping with Louis-Philippe's position at the beginning of his reign. It portrays a young Napoleon in the early phase of his career. Writing about this work in 1851 after the fall of Louis-Philippe but before Louis Napoleon's coup brought him to the throne as Napoleon III, Gustave Planche remarked:

> The costume of the General, on his return from Egypt, lends itself most happily to the exigencies of sculpture. . . . The pale, thin face of the General is suited to statuary. . . . The long coat, the rolling collar, the lapels spread upon the

Fig. 58. *General Bonaparte.*

chest, the distinctive marks of the military costume of the Directory could not be compared with the imperial mantle. . . . The statuette of General Bonaparte could easily become a monumental statue, and the author, in enlarging it, would have to make little or no change.[10]

Barye's other treatments of Napoleon at later stages in his reign, including a monumental equestrian in Roman imperial dress, were not executed until after Louis Napoleon became emperor.[11]

Three historical subjects—*Charles VI*, *Charles VII*, and *Gaston de Foix*—while reflective of the troubador style then so popular in French art,[12] portray individuals with close ties to the house of Orléans. Barye's interest in this type of romantic subject was recognized by his contemporaries. Writing shortly after the sculptor's death, Charles Blanc observed:

> Barye would not have belonged to his time if he had not evoked the characters and scenes of the Middle Ages. . . . These works bear witness to his careful study of every detail affecting his art. He took note of the ethnology, the manners and customs and of all the characteristics of different epochs. He made himself familiar with the faces and figures of history. . . . The forms and faces of his heroes were those of the times in which they lived. . . . Charles VII, sitting imperiously upon a richly caparisoned horse which seems to paw the ground, might be a copy in miniature of a monument of the fifteenth century.[13]

Barye, of course, was not alone among sculptors of small bronzes to deal with such themes. For example, Jean-François-Théodore Gechter executed *Francis I Hunting* in 1843.[14] Yet Barye's selection of these particular personages was probably due to more than just the current artistic interest in subjects drawn from the Middle Ages.

Commissioned by Louis-Philippe's daughter, Princess

Fig. 57. *Peasant of the Middle Ages.*

51

Fig. 59. *Charles VII Victorious.*

Fig. 60. *Gaston de Foix.*
Walters Art Gallery, Baltimore.

Marie-Christine of Orléans,[15] and shown at the Salon of 1833, *Charles VI Surprised in the Forest of Mans* (fig. 54) depicts an encounter between the king and a beggar in the woods, which supposedly precipitated Charles' periodic insanity. Madness was a subject of special interest to the Romantics, and several artists had treated this particular episode as well as other events in Charles' life.[16] Barye's approach is certainly sympathetic. Nevertheless, the portrayal of the subject, while emphasizing the human side of a king, was not an argument for hereditary monarchy.

During Charles VI's reign, Louis, Duke of Orléans, became one of his brother's chief ministers and founder of the house of Valois-Orléans, which under Louis XII succeeded to the French throne. Louis-Philippe was not a descendant of this house but rather of the Bourbon-Orléans line founded in the seventeenth century by Philippe, brother of Louis XIV. Still, Charles VI played an important part in the history of the Orléanist branch of the ruling dynasty. In Barye's sculpture of Charles VI, the young king is startled into a state of insanity and therefore incompetence by a beggar, who perhaps symbolizes the common people. The fact that Louis-Philippe succeeded another Charles following a popular uprising may well have been a contributing factor in the selection of such an unusual story.

*Charles VII Victorious* and *Gaston de Foix* (figs. 59, 60) were both created around 1839. It has been noted that the statue *Charles VII* depicts a youth riding a pony rather than a mature ruler mounted on a steed.[17] Charles VII, who succeeded his father to the throne in 1422, became Dauphin in 1417 at the age of fourteen upon the death of his older brother. Barye's statue seems to portray Charles at this early stage of his life.

Due to treaties Charles VI made with Henry V of England, Charles VII's claim to the French throne was in dispute. With the aid of Joan of Arc, the young king liberated a besieged Orléans in 1429. His coronation at Rheims eventually led to the reunification of France. As the liberator of Orléans, Charles VII had a connection to the city associated with the royal house of the Citizen King. Charles' further role as a unifier—through the person of Joan of Arc, the French people had called on him to lead the country to victory—would have appealed to Louis-Philippe, who was himself called to the throne at a time when France was beset with political factions that ranged from Bourbonists to republicans. Like Napoleon, Charles VII embodied sentiments of nationalism, but unlike Napoleon and like Louis-Philippe, he had a legitimate right to rule France.

*Gaston de Foix* depicts the young son of Marie of Orléans, sister of Louis XII, who died in the battle of Ravenna after a successful military operation in Italy. Also called Duke of Nemours, Gaston bore the same title as Louis-Philippe's second oldest son. Ary Scheffer, who frequently portrayed the king and his family, painted the subject of Gaston de Foix's death in 1824.

52

Fig. 61. *Duke of Orléans.*

(The canvas is in Versailles.) This allusion to the military glory achieved in foreign lands by a member of one of the former houses of Orléans was particularly appropriate to a regime then engaged in adventurism in North Africa and Asia.

The equestrian statue *Duke of Orléans* (fig. 61) is the most direct allusion to the Orléanist regime of all Barye's figurative pieces. A sympathetic portrait of one of the artist's first major patrons, the small bronze depicts the youthful heir to the throne around 1840, when the artist had just finished the *surtout*, and shortly before the duke's untimely death from a freak carriage accident in 1842. The military pose obviously refers to Barye's own recent equestrian portraits discussed above as well as to the duke's military activities and to his lineage, real and metaphoric.

Writing of Barye's statuette in 1851, Planche observed, ''The military costume of our own time is far from affording the same resources to the sculptor as the costumes of the fifteenth and sixteenth centuries. . . . Still M. Barye seems to have found the way to respect the uniform while bending it to his purpose. . . . It is too often that horsemen dressed in a military uniform

resemble manikins; the *Duke of Orléans* of M. Barye is supple and alive.''[18] Dressed in full military attire, the young man looks out as if reviewing his troops. Yet his sensitivity and thoughtfulness, along with the liberal tendencies that undoubtedly contributed to his popularity, are evident in the gentle gaze and soft features, which are accented by the somewhat casual tilt of the hat.

Produced about the same time, *Equestrienne in 1830 Dress* (fig. 62) may well be a portrait of the duke's wife, Hélène of Mecklembourg-Schwerin, completed shortly after their marriage in 1837.[19] Presumably Barye would have been happy to undertake a portrait of his young patron's wife. Moreover, if the duke had lived to succeed his father, the two works would have been popular items in the sculptor's repertoire.

The riding costume was identified in Barye's 1865 catalogue as being from 1830, some seven years before the duke's marriage. This reference to a specific year for the style of clothing may have been added to the work's description in the sculptor's last catalogue to make an association between the lady depicted and the Revolution of 1830, which brought Louis-Philippe to the

**Fig. 62.** *Equestrienne in 1830 Dress.*

throne. Unfortunately, the identity of the horsewoman remains conjectural. Although *Equestrienne* and *Duke of Orléans* complement each other visually, nowhere are they identified as pendants.

*Equestrienne* was called *Amazone* by Barye. The phrase, not uncommon at the time, was used to denote a strong, noble horsewoman, in keeping with the classical allusion to the mythological female warriors of ancient Scythia. In *A Murky Business*, Balzac characterizes the well-born heroine of his tale set in the early Napoleonic period in terms that almost describe Barye's contemporary visualization of the type: "Her Amazonian qualities were concealed behind a mask of utter femininity and fragility. She had great sensibility of heart but mentally she was a woman of virile determination and stoical firmness."[20]

Other artists, including Géricault and Delacroix, treated the theme of the modern Amazon, and Barye was familiar with some of these representations.[21] In the statuette, the heavy drapery of the skirt reveals the shape of the right calf, adding a touch of sensual femininity to this otherwise proper and restrained image of a galant young woman. Whether a portrait of the Duchess of Orléans or not, the lady with her cool demeanor and confident control of her mount is in every way a worthy

companion for the statue of the elegant and assured young duke.

Barye later created two pendant equestrian genre pieces—*Huntsman, Louis XV Period* and *Caucasian Warrior* (figs. 63, 64)—which provide interesting contrasts in subject and tone. He also returned to one of the hunt groups of the *surtout* for *Peasant of the Middle Ages* (fig. 57).[22] Far removed in time and locale from the French public of the mid-nineteenth century, the equestrian figures, perhaps conceived around the period of the Crimean War, seem to speak for the pleasures of peace and the threat of conflict; for the harmless pastimes of civilized nations and the warlike postures of non-Western societies. Even the *Peasant*, when divorced from the hunting context, takes on a threatening aspect with his aggressive stance.

Although small in number, the equestrians Barye produced in the 1830s and early 1840s seem to be a unified group of images. With little documentary information on the sculptor or his attitudes at the time he produced these pieces, however, any interpretation of them is speculative.[23] Yet it can be argued that not only do several of these pieces deal directly with Orléanist themes, but also all may have been created to serve the cause of a regime for which Barye produced some of his finest work.

Fig. 63. *Huntsman, Louis XV Period.*

Fig. 64. *Caucasian Warrior.*

## NOTES

I wish to acknowledge Trudi Y. Ludwig, whose preliminary observations on Barye's historical genre sculptures in Professor Robinson's graduate seminar served as the springboard for this paper. I also wish to thank Claudia Taylor, a summer intern at the Corcoran, for researching some of the subjects.

1  The exceptions are: three versions of Napoleon; the pendants *Huntsman, Louis XV Period* and *Caucasian Warrior*; and *Peasant of the Middle Ages*, which also is the only nonequestrian work. The last three are illustrated and discussed briefly below. For illustrations of the statues of Napoleon, see F2-4 in Stuart Pivar, *The Barye Bronzes: A Catalogue Raisonné* (Woodbridge, Suffolk, 1974), 52–54.

2  The commissions for the Duke of Orléans and Duke of Montpensier are mentioned in "Barye and the French Sculptural Tradition" and in other essays in this catalogue.

3  Charles Rosen and Henri Zerner, *Romanticism and Realism: The Mythology of Nineteenth-Century Art* (New York, 1984), 190.

4  *A Cavalier* is illustrated as F55 in Pivar, *Barye Bronzes*, 94.

5  Eugène Guillaume, "Introduction," in Roger Ballu, *L'Oeuvre de Barye* (Paris, 1890), xxiii.

6  George Louis Leclerc, Count de Buffon, *Natural History, General and Particular*, trans. William Smellie (20 vols.; London, 1812), V, 12. Buffon's monumental study, serially published in France between 1749 and 1804, went through numerous editions and translations.

7  Glenn F. Benge, *Antoine-Louis Barye: Sculptor of Romantic Realism* (University Park, PA, 1984), 145; also see Michael Marrinan, *Painting Politics for Louis-Philippe: Art and Ideology in Orléanist France, 1830–1848* (New Haven and London, 1988), 225, n. 115.

8  For a discussion on Bonapartism and Louis-Philippe, see Marrinan, *Painting Politics*, especially pt. III, 141–200.

9  For a discussion of the Salle of 1830 at Versailles, see *ibid.*, 57–66.

10  Gustave Planche, "Barye," in William Thompson Walters, comp., *Antoine-Louis Barye from the French of Various Critics* (Baltimore, 1885), 95. Planche's article originally appeared in *Revue des Deux Mondes*, 3 (July 1, 1851), 47–75.

11  See n. 1 above.

12  June Hargrove, "The Public Monument," in *The Romantics to Rodin: French Nineteenth-Century Sculpture from North American Collections* (Los Angeles, 1980), 24; also see Gert Schiff, "The Sculpture of the *Style Troubadour*," *Arts Magazine*, 58, no. 2 (Summer 1984), 102–10.

13  Charles Blanc, "The Exhibition of Barye's Works at the Ecole des Beaux-Arts," in Walters, *Barye*, 56. Blanc's remarks were published in the catalogue for the memorial exhibition.

14  For an illustration, see Schiff, *Style Troubadour*, 104.

15  Princess Marie-Christine of Orléans married Duke Alexandre of Wurttemberg in 1837; she died two years later. The youngest daughter of Louis-Philippe, she was a sculptor herself. Her most famous work, *Joan of Arc* (1836), deals with a subject from the same general period as *Charles VI*. A painting of the princess in her studio in the Tuileries (1842) by Prosper Lafaye, preserved at Versailles, includes Barye's statue on the left side of the room.

16  Schiff, "Style Troubadour," 106–107; also see Isabelle Leroy-Jay Lemaistre, "Le sentiment romantique," in *La Sculpture Française au XIXᵉ Siècle* (Paris, 1986), 319.

17  Benge, *Barye: Sculptor*, 148; also Schiff, "Style Troubadour," 108.

18  Quoted in Walters, *Barye*, 94.

19  An annotated illustration from a sales catalogue at the Hôtel Drouot in the documentation files of the Musée d'Orsay states that this statuette is a portrait of the Duchess, but the identification has not been corroborated by other contemporary sources or visual evidence. The figure, however, does bear a resemblance to known portraits of the Duchess. I wish to thank Frédéric Chappey for providing information on this piece.

20  Honoré de Balzac, *A Murky Business*, trans. Herbert J. Hunt (Harmondsworth, Middlesex, England, 1985), 59. The story was serialized early in 1841 and first published as a book the following year.

21  Benge, *Barye: Sculptor*, 102. For a close parallel, see Géricault's pen-and-ink drawing reproduced in Klaus Berger, *Géricault: Drawings and Watercolors* (New York, 1946), 30, fig. 36. There was even a group of noblewomen, modern Amazon warriors, who fought in 1832 for the Duchess of Berry in an abortive effort to oust Louis-Philippe and place her son, the Bourbon heir, on the throne.

22  All three works appear as new models in Barye's catalogue of 1865, suggesting that they were created sometime after his previous catalogue appeared in 1855. See Pivar, *Barye Bronzes*, 271.

23  In his journal of May 26, 1855, Delacroix refers to Barye as a "republican," but this was just a few years after Napoleon III had consolidated his power. See Eugène Delacroix, *The Journal of Eugène Delacroix*, ed. Hubert Wellington, trans. Lucy Norton (1951; rpt. Oxford, 1980), 463.

Fig. 65. *Nine Light Candelabrum.*

56

# VII

# Barye's

# DECORATIVE ARTS

Marcia R. Schifanelli

Antoine-Louis Barye's artistic roots were in the decorative arts. The son of a silversmith, Barye served a four-year apprenticeship (1809–13) to the metalworker Fourier and in the late 1820s made small gold and silver objects for the goldsmith Jacques Henri Fauconnier. As a sculptor who created functional pieces, Barye helped to establish the importance of the decorative arts at a time when they were relegated to a lower rank of artistic creativity by the Societé des Artistes Français.

Barye's six sales catalogues, published from 1847 to 1865, include candelabra, candlesticks, card receivers, fire fenders, incense burners, and inkwells.[1] Almost half of his approximately thirty-five designs for functional objects appeared in the first catalogue of 1847. Nine distinct forms are in the Corcoran's collection: two pair of candelabra, a single candelabrum, four single candlesticks, and two card receivers. They are representative of Barye's designs for stemmed objects, a category that constitutes seventy percent of his *oeuvre* of domestic items.

The modest prices listed in the catalogue suggest that virtually all his utilitarian pieces were created for the middle class. A pair of ornate figural candelabra, probably commissioned by the Duke of Montpensier, constitutes an exception.[2] Numbers occasionally inscribed on the base of an object denote how many examples were made from an original mold. In some cases, the numbers are high, indicating a strong market for a particular item.[3]

Most pieces in demand were created in the Romantic style, a type of design that was in many ways formu-

lated as a reaction to the mode of decoration that had prevailed during the Napoleonic period. Motifs from that era were often classical in nature and referred to Greek and Roman art. Favorite elements included winged figures and emblems of victory as well as eagles and lions. While the Neoclassical style of the First Empire was characterized by an elegant severity, the Romantic style was marked by an exuberant eclecticism. Motifs appropriated from many periods were often combined into a single piece. Design elements borrowed from nature or exotic cultures were also favored.

In many ways, Barye's objects conformed to the contemporary fashion of the Romantic style. Richly decorated, they are eclectic in their allusions, and yet their effect is singular. Etruscan, Roman, Renaissance, Baroque, Rococo, and Islamic motifs occur regularly on objects in the Corcoran's collection, as do plant and animal elements. The sheer variety of sources speaks unmistakably of the nineteenth century.

Curvilinear forms, frequently derived from nature, were recurring motifs in the period. Barye's works are no exception, although his curves are restrained. So, too, is his use of decoration, which never overwhelms the object. Instead, the softly painted bronze reinforces the object's dignified effect. His schemes are carefully considered, and potentially disparate motifs are subtly integrated, as seen in the candlestick with medallion that combines Classical and Islamic elements (fig. 70).

A masterful pair of figural candelabra (fig. 65) created in the early 1840s[4] once formed a garniture together with *Roger and Angelica on the Hippogriff* (fig. 50). Miss-

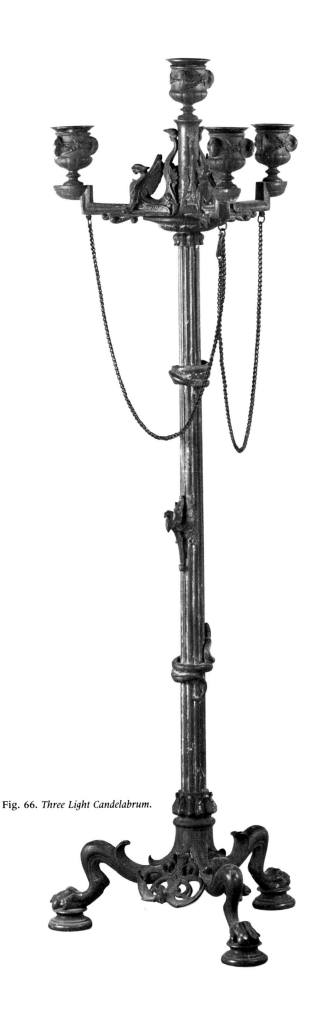

Fig. 66. *Three Light Candelabrum.*

ing from the Corcoran's candelabra, however, is a top segment that consists of a representation of the Three Graces. The ensemble was probably created for the Duke of Montpensier, who commissioned it presumably because of Barye's work on the elaborate bronze *surtout de table* for his brother, the Duke of Orléans. The candelabra appeared in Barye's first catalogue of 1847. Individual elements were later offered separately. Each of the three goddesses that adorn the piece were cast as small sculptures, two of which, *Juno* and *Minerva* (figs. 52, 53), are in the Corcoran's collection.

Part of a long tradition of figural lighting devices produced since antiquity, the candelabra by Barye exhibit Mannerist influences in the proportions of the goddesses and in their twisting poses and small heads. His ideas for these figures, as well as for the chimeras and grotesques, may have come from sixteenth- and seventeenth-century designs in general and more specifically from Mannerist illustrations in early editions of Ariosto's *Orlando Furioso*. First published in 1516, that epic poem tells the story of Roger and Angelica. Significantly, the elongated figures in the decorative borders of these illustrations assume twisting, contemplative poses, as do Barye's goddesses, and grotesque masks appear in the frames. Other features of the candelabra recall antique and Renaissance sources, some of which were readily available to Barye through plaster casts in the Louvre and objects in the Caylus collection.[5]

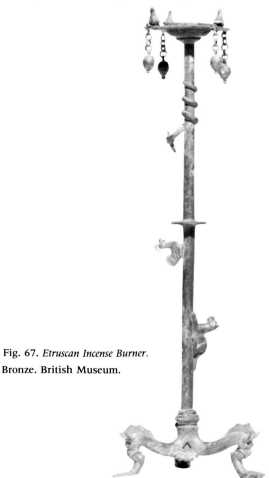

Fig. 67. *Etruscan Incense Burner.*
Bronze. British Museum.

At the base of each candelabrum are three fully sculpted figures, Juno, Minerva, and Venus, the three goddesses whose competition for the title of the fairest, according to mythology, ignited the Trojan War. Portrayed as thoughtful and restrained, each is shown with her attribute: Juno, a peacock; Minerva, an owl; and Venus, a dolphin. Together, they support an urn-shaped knop embellished with three chimeras. Each candelabrum's nine arms are decorated with acanthus leaves and tendrils resembling those found on Rococo candelabra of the previous century.[6] Entwined figures of the Three Graces once formed the finial to this elaborate sculptural tribute to ideal female beauty and grace, a major theme of Ariosto's chivalric romance.

A pair of three-light candelabra (fig. 66), ca. 1845, reveal a strong Etruscan influence in their long, slender stems decorated with griffins and coiled snakes. (The Corcoran's two are missing finials in the forms of storks.) Some of the motifs are reminiscent of elements found on bronze incense burners, ca. 300–250 B.C. from the Vulcan province of Italy (fig. 67). Similar works in the Louvre may have influenced Barye. Perhaps he was drawn to Etruscan objects because of their variety of plant and animal motifs. Except for the fact that the candlestick is much larger than the incense burner, Barye closely followed a classical prototype, making only minor changes, such as the addition of arms and sockets. Unlike the candelabra he designed for the Duke of Montpensier, which combined Classical, Mannerist, and Rococo elements, these show a conscious historicism in their close imitation of an Etruscan form.

Barye's candlestick with panther heads (fig. 68) appeared in his first catalogue and therefore predates 1847. His training as a goldsmith and jeweler is particularly evident in the delicately modeled animal forms that cover the surface. Owls with stylized wings circle the base, and panther heads in relief adorn the bold knop of the stem, which itself derives from the seventeenth-century Venetian glassware then enjoying a revival among French glassmakers.[7]

Designed as a receptacle on which a visitor left a calling card, Barye's card receiver is in the form of a raised salver (fig. 69). Grape clusters in relief decorate the shallow bowl. The stem, cast from the same mold as the candlestick with panther heads, exemplifies Barye's practice of utilizing interchangeable parts. He probably learned this method as a jeweler's apprentice, since his job included casting small pieces and making decorative stampings for use in various combinations. Adapting the method of sand casting to bronze objects was undoubtedly done to reduce costs and prices. His simple, easily reproduced forms still allowed for a singular style and high artistic standards.

Although such technological developments as sand casting facilitated the duplication of objects and individual elements, a considerable amount of time was still required to make each mold. To create a plain object

Fig. 68. *Candlestick, Cup Form.*

Fig. 69. *Card Receiver.*

59

Fig. 70. *Candlestick, Greek Style.*

Fig. 71. *Coin, Decadrachm,* ca. 413-357 B.C.
Virginia Museum of Fine Arts, Williams Fund.

would have been simpler, but the piece would have lacked the vital elements of Barye's style—penetrating observation and intricate, jewellike detail—and scarcely would have appealed to his audience. Fortunately, Barye's sense of harmony and proportion allowed him

to mix parts with great success, and each design retains a sense of distinction.

First appearing in the catalogue of 1855, the candlestick with medallion (fig. 70) shows two classical heads in profile, each slightly different, enclosed in a beaded circle. Since the motif is reminiscent of those found on Greco-Roman coins, it can be assumed that Barye was familiar with such ancient pieces as the coin of Syracuse (ca. 400 B.C.) that contains a representation of the nymph Arethusa (fig. 71). Also part of the classical vocabulary are the series of flat, circular forms, or disks, above and below the medallion. Barye was eclectic in his references. The arches that appear on the knops on both ends of the stem, along with the radiating pointed elements on the base, may have been borrowed from Islamic decoration. This mixture of Classical and Islamic motifs was perhaps prompted by a contemporary development. As Rome had once defeated Carthage, a North African empire that included parts of Sicily, France had subdued a North African nation. In 1830, provoked by attacks on European shipping, France sent an expedition to Algeria. The country was colonized by the late 1840s, but uprisings continued throughout the next decade. Perhaps in his decoration of this piece, Barye was making reference to the imperial ambitions of Louis-Philippe and his successor, Napoleon III.

More than simply a side interest, Barye's work in the decorative arts reveals another side of his artistic personality. While his sculptures often exude a sense of emotion and drama, his functional pieces show a high degree of reserve and refinement. The eight years Barye spent in Fauconnier's workshop instilled in him a love of detail and a sensitivity to scale. These characteristics distinguish his entire *oeuvre,* his animal sculptures as well as his decorative pieces.

### NOTES

1 Glenn F. Benge, *Antoine-Louis Barye: Sculptor of Romantic Realism* (University Park, PA, 1984). Targeting a large group of potential purchasers, the catalogues contain brief descriptions of objects along with dimensions and prices.

2 *Ibid.,* 162. Benge notes that although the early literature indicates that the candelabra were commissioned by Montpensier, no documentation has been found to prove this.

3 There are no numbers on the Corcoran objects.

4 Recent studies date the piece to 1840; however, an early catalogue of the Corcoran's collection gives a date of 1846. The latter date is plausible since the candelabra, along with *Roger and Angelica on the Hippogriff,* may have been ordered on the occasion of the marriage of Montpensier and Louisa, the sister of the Queen of Spain.

5 See Benge, *Barye: Sculptor,* 152. While no specific source can be identified, there is a suggestion of antiquity in the palmettes and acanthus swags on the base, and of the Renaissance in the chimeras that encircle the stem. See also Benge, *ibid.,* 152, for a discussion of the piece, and a source in the Caylus collection that may have inspired the pose of *Minerva.* Barye would also have been familiar with contemporary books on design illustrating traditional styles and motifs. See, for example, Charles Norman, *Le Guide de Ornemaniste* (Paris,1826).

6 For an illustration of a Rococo candelabrum, see Waith Dennis, *Three Centuries of French Domestic Silver* (New York, 1967), 91.

7 Dan Klein and Ward Lloyd, eds.,*The History of Glass* (London,1984),18

# THE WATERCOLORS OF

# Antoine-Louis Barye

Martina Roudabush Norelli

Antoine-Louis Barye is well known today for his bronze sculptures. During his career, however, he also enjoyed a fine reputation as a painter in watercolor and oil. The three watercolors in the Corcoran Gallery of Art's collection—*Two Lions Resting* (fig. 72), *Tiger Searching for a Track* (fig. 73), and *Tiger Hunt* (fig. 74)—are among the 217 documented watercolors by Barye,[1] and compositionally and thematically, they are representative of his *oeuvre* in the medium. Lions and tigers were common subjects for Barye, with a single animal or two animals being the most prevalent. *Two Lions Resting* and *Tiger Searching for a Track* are therefore typical of his composition; *Tiger Hunt*, however, is another matter. One of two watercolors of this subject (the other is in the Baltimore Museum of Art, fig. 75), it is unusual in both style and composition.

A prolific painter as well as sculptor and printmaker, Barye exhibited watercolors from the earliest years of his career.[2] Like many of the artists of this period, he worked in a variety of media. Several of Barye's contemporaries—his friend Eugène Delacroix, for example—were painters, printmakers, and sometimes sculptors.[3]

Hundreds of sketches document Barye's insatiable curiosity and his penchant for capturing not only the spirited movement of animals but also their anatomical details.[4] Many of Barye's drawings date from a period in the late 1820s and early 1830s when he was close to Delacroix.[5] The two artists sketched together at the zoo in the Jardin des Plantes and also witnessed postmortem examinations of zoo animals. In addition, they shared drawings, knowledge, and books. For example, the Cor-

coran's *Tiger Hunt* is probably based on an illustration in Edward Turner Bennett's *The Tower Menagerie*, which was in Delacroix's library. The tailpiece for the chapter "The Asiatic Elephant" bears a striking resemblance to Barye's watercolor (fig. 76). Tailpieces for the chapters on "Anaconda" and "Rattlesnake" have elements that appear in other Barye works.[6]

Delacroix and Barye were also greatly influenced by Peter Paul Rubens, especially by his hunt scenes and his treatment of horses. Both made sketches of Rubens' works, either from the oils or from prints after the paintings.[7] Delacroix owned a group of prints after Rubens' hunt paintings, and as early as 1827 sketches derived directly from these prints appeared in that artist's sketchbooks. As this was the precise time when Barye and Delacroix were close, one can reasonably assume that Barye was aware of these same sources.

Barye left little documentation of his non-sculptural work, and none of the watercolors was dated. Although he exhibited his watercolors early in his career, after his break with the Salon in 1837 they were apparently exhibited and sold privately. Even when shown publicly, they were often listed as a group of works and not identified individually by title. Nevertheless, it would seem that the watercolors were very popular with collectors. George Lucas, who noted in his journals numerous visits to Barye's studio with William Walters and others,[8] not only purchased watercolors directly from Barye but also acquired several at the estate sale of Barye's works at the Hôtel Drouot in 1875, including *Two Lions Resting* and *Tiger Hunt*.

Although Barye's watercolors were highly valued—some costing more than several bronzes[9]—the medium of watercolor had not been popular in France in the early nineteenth century. The change in attitude seemed to coincide with the Romantic period, the decisive factor probably being a growth in French awareness of English achievements in the medium.[10] Théodore Géricault and Delacroix were especially important in transmitting English ideas to France. Both had spent time in England, and both admired British watercolors.

In 1829 the term "aquarelliste" (watercolor painter) was first used, yet in 1842 the author of an article in *L'Artiste* still observed that "watercolour has attained an importance and a degree of perfection far greater than one might have expected."[11] Barye, however, was praised in a review of the watercolors in the 1833 Salon for giving animals the "same life and the same truth in his watercolors as in his plasters."[12] With its fluidity and apparent spontaneity, watercolor became an effective medium by which Barye could readily capture the vitality, and often the violence, of his animal subjects. Although only twenty-six of his watercolors depict animals in combat, the preference for carnivores as subjects underscores Barye's interest in animals of prey. More than half of his 217 watercolors are of large cats, including the two scenes of tiger hunts.[13]

In all Barye's watercolors the animals are more important than the backgrounds. Often the animals do not seem to be integrated into the landscapes that surround them but instead stand out boldly within their settings. The dark outlining of an animal's contours sets it in relief, giving a three-dimensionality to Barye's subjects that is sculptural in feeling. Barye's watercolors, through their uncluttered compositions, have a greater sense of focus than the more complex compositions of Rubens, Géricault, and Delacroix.

The backgrounds of his watercolors and oils are based on the forest of Fontainebleau.[14] Barye never traveled outside France or further from Paris than Fontainebleau. The landscape around Barbizon, particularly the desolate areas of Belle Croix and Apremont, became his source for the "rocks sticking up from the sandy soil, the scanty, twisted vegetation, the heavy skies leaning low and charged with rain" that typify the settings of his watercolors.[15] Although Barye is often praised for providing realistic "environments" for his bronzes, in his paintings the landscapes are, for the most part, incidental backdrops to the animal. Both the manner of presenting the animal within the landscape and the animal's central placement within the composition underscore the fact that the animal alone is the reason for his paintings.

These watercolors were clearly intended as finished works to be exhibited and sold, not as sketches for

**Fig. 72.** *Two Lions Resting.*

**Fig. 73.** *Tiger Searching for a Track.*

sculptures or oils. One of the few watercolors that bears a direct resemblance to a sculpture is *Tiger Hunt*. Unfortunately, since neither of the watercolors belonging to the Corcoran Gallery or to the Baltimore Museum of Art is dated, it cannot be definitively stated whether either of them preceded, followed, or originated from the same period as the sculptural group that Barye created in 1836 for the Duke of Orléans (fig. 22). Since the two watercolors do not reproduce the sculpture exactly, it is possible that Barye tried out variant compositions in these works.

There is no documentation of Barye's study of the watercolor medium. His dark, relatively subdued palette and straightforward compositions, however, would indicate that his interest in watercolors derived as much from his friendship with the Barbizon painters as from his exposure to the watercolors by Delacroix. The smoky atmosphere of Barye's paintings is quite similar to that found in the paintings by Honoré Daumier, Jean-François Millet, and Théodore Rousseau.[16] *Tiger Hunt* appears far more transparent in medium than other watercolors by Barye. It and the watercolor of the same subject in the Baltimore Museum have lost some of their surface contrast through light damage, which has caused the support and pigments to discolor.

The majority of Barye's watercolors were executed with pigment-rich watercolors in a gelatin glue binder. Mottled effects and occasional shiny areas within the paintings suggest the use of this type of medium. Areas of graininess and smoothness indicate variations in the thoroughness with which the pigment was dispersed in the binder, causing it, when diluted, to settle on the surface of the paper in irregular patterns.[17] Théophile Gautier described the watercolors—both admirable and laborious—as "no ordinary water-colours, the brush [having] the firmness of the sculptor's tool. . . . There are tones which come too near the clay of his daily use; and his distances want air; but every single water-colour, even the least successful, bears the print of the lion's paw."[18] Gautier's description points to the difficulty that Barye had in maintaining the clarity of the colors in his paintings. In many instances, Barye worked the medium to the point of muddiness, thus warranting Gautier's description of the tones as resembling the clay Barye used. At the same time, Gautier recognized the quality that made these watercolors so popular—Barye's uncanny ability to project the essence of the raw power of animals. Consequently, the watercolors were as sought after as Barye's sculptures.

Following Barye's death, the Ecole des Beaux-Arts held a memorial exhibition in November 1875. Displayed with the 349 bronzes and plasters were at least seventy watercolors, all but three of animal subjects; ninety-three oils, almost all landscapes; and 137 drawings and sketches, nearly all animal subjects. These impressive numbers point to the fact that Barye's *oeuvre* cannot be fully understood without an examination of his watercolors, paintings, drawings, and prints. Even within his lifetime, critics acclaimed these works. Philippe Burty in 1859 described Barye as "one of the

Fig. 74. *Tiger Hunt.*

premier watercolorists of our epoch" and further stated that "the nobility of the drawings and the severe search for the contour makes these watercolors the most elevated works of art."[19] The following year Gautier described Barye as a "remarkable painter" and cited only Delacroix and Méry as artists capable of painting

tigers with the strength of those by Barye.[20] Fourteen years after Barye's death, Philippe de Chennevières acknowledged Barye's versatility among nineteenth-century French artists by calling him "the most learned and most powerful of the sculptor-painter-draftsmen."[21]

Fig. 75. *Tiger Chase.* George A. Lucas Collection of The Maryland Institute, College of Art, on indefinite loan to The Baltimore Museum of Art.

Fig. 76. William Harvey, "Tiger Hunt" from Edward Turner Bennett, *The Tower Menagerie*. **Smithsonian Institution.**

## NOTES

1   Charles O. Zieseniss, *Les Aquarelles de Barye: Étude critiques et catalogue raisonné* (Paris, 1956). See entries A43, B41, and E10 for the three watercolors owned by the Corcoran Gallery.

2   Barye included watercolors as well as his sculpture in both the 1833 and 1834 Paris Salons. Zieseniss, *Les Aquarelles*, 11, states that Barye exhibited watercolors in the 1831 as well as the 1833 and 1834 Salons. The 1831 Salon catalogue, however, lists only "90—Un portrait" and "91—Etudes d'animaux; dessins." The 1833 Salon catalogue indicates six watercolors by title (numbers 94 to 99), and the 1834 Salon catalogue lists "Etudes d'animaux; aquarelles" under number 74, but does not indicate the number of works or their titles. Barye was also a painter in oils, but these works were less well known during his lifetime. The oils were often quite small and usually of a single animal in a landscape or more often solely of a landscape.

3   See Zieseniss, *Les Aquarelles*, 36, and Eugène Delacroix, *Selected Letters, 1813–1863* (New York, 1970), 151.

4   See George Heard Hamilton, "The Origin of Barye's Tiger Hunt," *Art Bulletin*, 18 (June 1936), 250, n. 7, and William R. Johnston, "The Barye Collection of the Walters Art Gallery, Baltimore," *Apollo*, 50 (November 1974), 407, for discussions of the 348 drawings at the Walters Art Gallery; also Marvin C. Ross in "Some Drawings by A. L. Barye," *Magazine of Art*, 43 (April 1950), 142–43.

5   Delacroix, *Selected Letters*, 151. See also Henry Eckford, "Antoine-Louis Barye," *Century Magazine*, 31, no. 4 (February 1886), 485.

6   Lee Johnson, "Delacroix, Barye and 'The Tower Menagerie': An English Influence on French Romantic Animal Pictures," *Burlington Magazine*, 106, no. 738 (September 1964), 416–17. He refers to a log Delacroix kept of books and works lent to friends. The log not only documents Delacroix's loan of "croquis de chevaux" in late 1829 to Barye but also indicates that Delacroix owned a set of the illustrations for *The Tower Menagerie*, published in London in 1829.

7   See Glenn F. Benge, *Antoine-Louis Barye: Sculptor of Romantic Realism* (University Park, PA, 1984), fig. 182, a drawing after Rubens now in the Walters Art Gallery; and Eve Twose Kliman, "Delacroix's Lions and Tigers: A Link Between Man and Nature," *Art Bulletin*, 64, no. 3 (September 1982), 454. See also Frank Anderson Trapp, *The Attainment of Delacroix* (Baltimore, 1971), 212–13. He quotes Delacroix's analysis in 1847 of Pieter Claesz Soutman's prints after Rubens' hunt scenes.

8   See Lillian M. C. Randall, trans., *The Diary of George A. Lucas: An American Art Agent in Paris, 1857–1909* (2 vols; Princeton, 1979).

9   When William Walters acquired two watercolors for his collection in 1863, he paid 845 francs for the pair. Three years later, however, George Lucas purchased two bronzes and a pair of candlesticks for only 469 francs. *Tiger Hunt* was acquired by Lucas for 800 francs, and *Two Lions Resting* for 430 francs. A. Marmontel acquired *Tiger Searching for a Track* in 1898 at a sale at the Hôtel Drouot for 2,400 francs.

10   François Daulte, *French Watercolors of the Nineteenth Century* (New York, 1969), 11.

11   *Ibid.*, 12.

12   "Aquarelles," *L'Artiste*, 1st. ser., V (1833), 176. The reviewer states further that "these watercolors promise us beautiful paintings if Barye decides one day to paint animals on canvas." This could indicate that in 1833 Barye had not yet begun to paint in oils or merely that the reviewer did not know of them.

13   The watercolors of big cats include fifty of lions, fifty-two of tigers, and thirty watercolors of leopards, panthers, or civit cats. Barye painted small numbers of watercolors of animals such as vultures, bear, buffalo, and horses, but also thirty-five of deer, stag, or antelope, eleven of pythons, and ten of elephants.

14   Charles Saunier, *Barye* (New York, 1926), 55, 57.

15   *Ibid.*, 55. See also Charles Sprague Smith, *Barbizon Days* (New York, 1903), 15, on the landscape around Fontainebleau.

16   In 1841, Barye spent part of the summer with Rousseau, but by the 1860s he had rented his own cottage. See Saunier, *Barye*, 55–57, and Jean Bouret, *The Barbizon School and Nineteenth-Century French Landscape Painting* (Greenwich, CT, 1973), 117–20.

17   Much of the information regarding the media of the Corcoran's watercolors is derived from a visual examination of the works in 1987 by Katherine Eirk, a conservator. Corcoran Gallery records indicate that the varnish on the surface of *Tiger Searching for a Track* was added in April 1933; it has recently been removed.

18   Théophile Gautier, quoted in Saunier, *Barye*, 58.

19   Ph[ilippe] Burty, "Ventes d'Aquarelles, de Dessins et de Tableaux," *Gazette des Beaux-Arts*, 1 (February 1, 1859), 184, 185.

20   Théophile Gautier, "Exposition de Tableaux Modernes," *Gazette des Beaux-Arts*, 2nd ser., V (March 15, 1860), 324, 325.

21   Ph[ilippe] de Chennevières, "Exposition Retrospective des Dessins, 1789–1889," *Gazette des Beaux-Arts*, 3rd ser., II (August 1889), 143.

# Barye

## AND PATRONAGE

Lilien Filipovitch Robinson

Nineteenth-century sculptors generally looked to two primary sources for purchase of their work: the government (national or local) and the individual patron. From the beginning of the July Monarchy, the government's support of the artist increased, and it continued to do so throughout the Second Empire. The State dominated the education of the artist and played a crucial role in his employment.[1] Monumental works were primarily government commissions. The State held competitions for the design and execution of public monuments, and the competing sculptors faced a complicated system of reviews. Once a sculptor was selected, however, he was virtually guaranteed future assignments and recognition.[2]

Refurbishment activities in Paris under the Second Empire significantly expanded artistic programs, but in the process, the sculptor was subjected to increased State scrutiny and control. Moreover, politics and personality frequently affected selection.[3] Sculptors had another resource available to them—purchase by subscription. Funds for designated monuments were obtained from individuals as well as voted by local governments.[4]

Although Barye did receive government patronage, private patrons, both aristocrat and bourgeois, formed the major source of his long-term support. This market was particularly interested in the small-scale works that Barye produced in abundance and that made his reputation. During the July Monarchy he attracted the attention of aristocrats, particularly members of the Orléans family, including the king and his two sons, the Duke of

Orléans and the Duke of Montpensier. Aristocrats, along with middle-class collectors, continued to dominate the art market into the Second Empire. France was undergoing a democratization of taste, and artists popular with the aristocracy were generally not distinguishable from the favorites of the middle class. Louis-Philippe's designation as the "bourgeois monarch" conveyed his artistic preferences as well. He favored the *juste-milieu* painters, who were so popular with the general Salon public. Similarly, the purchases by Napoleon III and members of the imperial family who had special interests in the arts (Empress Eugènie, Princess Mathilde, and Prince Napoleon) echoed general bourgeois selections. Despite a catholicity of taste, exemplified in a simultaneous acceptance of new developments and the revival of earlier styles, there was a definite orientation towards easy-to-understand subjects and technical virtuosity.[5]

A further insight into prevailing tastes can be gleaned from an examination of contemporary interiors.[6] For example, a room in the palace of the Duke of Morny combined rather formal authentic furnishings of several periods with more informal and intimate contemporary pieces. Family portraits were flanked by a collection of decorative objects and small sculptures, including Barye's *Tiger Devouring a Gavial*.[7] Concern for tradition seemed to coexist with a love of the modern.

The middle class, for its part, was fervently involved in the arts. Its members attended Salon openings, debated reviews and accounts of the state of the arts, and frequented the shops of art dealers, whose numbers were escalating. Perhaps the retention of traditional, legitimate styles was even more essential to this group than to the aristocracy. Eager to possess period furnishings and the works of master painters, they also supported modernity. They were delighted with new processes that facilitated the production of replicas and contemporary furnishings. At modest cost, this group could imitate the homes and life style of the aristocracy.[8]

In this context, the popularity of Barye's works becomes even more understandable. His middle-class public was captivated by subjects that excited the imagination and demonstrated the artist's technical skill. Moreover, his bronzes were financially accessible because of modern technology. Suitable in scale and clearly modern in feeling, they formed an excellent complement to the contemporary interior. For the devotees of science, the naturalistic accuracy of Barye's bronzes made them superior to earlier renderings.

The patronage of Barye expanded, especially during the decade of the 1860s. After his death in 1875, both his reputation and the sale of his works continued to increase.[9] Prices remained relatively modest during Barye's lifetime and even as late as the 1876 Hôtel Drouot sale of the contents of his studio.[10] In the next decade, however, a marked increase in prices for all categories of his work occurred.

While Barye's greatest European support was in France, his recognition was not limited to that country. In 1888, a critic bemoaned Barye's absence from public collections in England and thus the lack of opportunity for English sculptors to learn from him. At the same time, he indicated that Barye's "reputation is increasing year by year, and in France and America, at least he is fast nearing his proper place in popular esteem as the greatest sculptor of his generation."[11] British neglect of Barye is curious, given the English tradition of animal painting.[12]

In America, Barye's work was most enthusiastically collected during his life. The introduction and promotion of his work in the United States was in large measure due to two individuals, Barye's former student William Morris Hunt and the expatriate art dealer George Lucas. Hunt introduced Barye's works, along with those of the sculptor's Barbizon colleagues, to numerous wealthy Bostonians. He especially promoted the work of Millet and Barye, both of whom he considered the most important artists of their time.[13] It was through George Lucas, a former Baltimorean, however, that several of the most important American collections of Barye's works were acquired. In his role as art agent and dealer from 1861 to 1908, Lucas contacted well-known artists in Paris, including Barye. Acting on behalf of American collectors, he purchased their works, many of which later became the basis for public collections in Boston, New York, Philadelphia, Baltimore, and Washington, D.C. Among American collectors who came to

Paris to consult with Lucas where John T. Johnston, Cornelius Vanderbilt, William H. Vanderbilt, Robert Garrett, Cyrus J. Lawrence, Frank Frick, Henry Walters, and William T. Walters.[14]

Lucas was also instrumental in assisting American art dealer Samuel P. Avery in his purchases. From 1865 to 1904, Avery promoted the works of European painters, sculptors, and printmakers. After his introduction to Lucas in 1867, Avery acquired works either on annual buying trips or through Lucas. In turn, he sold them to collectors such as John T. Johnston, William H. Vanderbilt, and others. It is likely that Avery's purchases of Barye's works were influenced by Lucas.[15]

Baltimorean collector Frank Frick made his own selections on a series of European trips from 1860 to 1909. Although a link to Lucas, Frick's childhood friend, also exists, some of his purchases, perhaps even his manner of collecting, may have been influenced by Lucas. Frick favored landscape and genre paintings by artists such as Felix Ziem, Auguste-Fréderic Albrecht Schenck, and Jules-Ernest Dévaux, all of whom were popular with middle-class French patrons.[16] He also repeatedly visited Barye's studio, making numerous purchases as early as 1860.[17]

Americans epitomized the democratization of collecting.[18] Unlike their European counterparts, they could neither take comfort in nor be hindered by an existing tradition of collecting. Additionally, they were subject to no preconceived notions of aristocratic monopoly over collecting. Industrialists, merchants, and bankers of established and recently acquired wealth were eager to emulate and surpass what was perceived to be a sophisticated European culture.

As indicated, these collectors shared a common denominator: George Lucas.[19] While employed as an engineer in New York City, he began to serve as an art agent for fellow Baltimoreans. By 1857, Lucas had turned his full attention to the arts and to assisting others in collecting. In that year he settled in Paris permanently and became absorbed in its art world during a period of unparalleled artistic activity. He purchased both for himself and on behalf of American collectors. His selections in painting varied, ranging from the work of Delacroix to animalier painting and landscapes of the Barbizon school.[20]

A dedicated and knowledgeable collector of paintings and prints at a time when interest in the latter was limited, Lucas was equally familiar with sculpture. By 1859, he was drawn to Barye, from whom he purchased works for other collectors and for himself.[21] It has been suggested that Lucas' background in engineering may have been the catalyst for his interest in the scientifically oriented Barye.[22] Whatever the impetus, Lucas' purchase of Barye's work remained constant.

Of all the American collectors assisted by Lucas, William Walters emerged the most strongly devoted to the art of Barye. He was also in large measure instrumental in insuring Barye's recognition in France. His contribution, as well as that of the committee he established, assured the construction in 1894 of a commemorative monument to Barye on the Boulevard Pont Sully in Paris. In addition, he initiated the purchase of an edition of Barye's four figural groups on the Louvre for Mount Vernon Place in Baltimore. Walters' interest in Barye began with an 1861 trip to Paris, after he had already amassed an impressive collection of works by other artists. His preference for realistic, technically fine, and frequently small-scale works must have predisposed him to Barye.[23]

Walters involvement in collecting was twofold—public and private. Following the success of several sales of his purchases at the Düsseldorf Gallery in New York City, he entered into a profitable business venture with Avery and Lucas, who made the selections. Purchases were financed by Walters and exhibited for sale in the Avery Gallery.[24] The venture proved profitable for all three parties due to the excellent American market.

On the private level, Walters methodically formed a major collection. Although it echoed current tastes, it primarily reflected his preference for the pleasant landscapes of the Barbizon school, intimate genre paintings by Édouard Frère and Ernest Meissonier, and sentimental works by Adolphe Bougereau and Charles Gleyre. After his introduction to Barye, Walters visited the sculptor's studio on subsequent trips, although he continued to employ Lucas as his agent to purchase Barye's sculptures and paintings.[25] He was determined to form a comprehensive collection of the artist's works, not only for his own enjoyment but also as a tribute to Barye's stature as an artist. In 1888, he completed the most important part of the collection, adding three hunt groups from the table decoration commissioned by the Duke of Orléans. Walters' collection of works by Barye was further expanded by his son Henry. In 1923, the latter was still purchasing bronzes by the master, particularly "early works not available in father's lifetime, or rare, even unique casts."[26]

While Walters clearly had personal interest in the arts, he also possessed a strong sense of public responsibility. He was intent on introducing a still artistically unaware public to the arts in general and to Barye in particular. In 1876, the Walters collection was made available for public viewing twice weekly. By 1884, a separate gallery wing had been added to the house. In the tradition of other American collectors, Walters used his fortune for the public benefit while he asserted his artistic preferences. In 1885, after a twenty-four-year friendship with Barye and ten years after the artist's death, Walters reflected on his collection, noting that he had acquired

> perhaps the most comprehensive collection of his [Barye's] works comprising some seventy to eighty characteristic examples of paintings in oil and watercolors, and of sculptures in bronze. A number of the watercolors were selected

from those he had set aside to be reserved during his life; a large proportion of the bronzes are those prepared with great care under his own hand, and used as *modèles*, from which casts were made. . . . The remainder are early impressions, and are now called proofs. . . .[27]

In 1869, Walters was selected by William Wilson Corcoran for membership on the Board of Trustees of the newly established Corcoran Gallery of Art. He was also appointed chairman of the acquisitions committee and given responsibility for the purchase of European art. In this capacity Walters furthered American appreciation of Barye's work. "As trustee of one of the Art Institutions of our country, I gave Barye a command in 1873 for a copy of every work he had produced in bronze. . . . To have been able to give this commission was one of the most agreeable acts of my life in relation to my art experience. . . ."[28] At the first public viewing of the Corcoran collection in 1874, Walters, who was described as possessing "superior taste and judgment in matters of art," was recognized for his role in the establishment of the capital city's impressive art collection.[29]

Corcoran, Walters' Washington counterpart, represents another aspect of American art patronage. For Corcoran, collecting appears to have been solidly linked to his broad philanthropic activities. Partnership in a successful banking firm permitted his active role in and financial support of numerous causes, most of which were associated with the city of Washington and many of which were related to education.[30]

At the onset of his collecting activities, Corcoran had neither an established interest in art nor direct links to the art world. His earliest purchases, made during an 1849 European trip, appear to have been based on the ad hoc advice of recent European contacts.[31] Judging from the list of his collection in 1874, his selections reflected current European taste for realistic landscapes, sentimental portraits, and genre scenes.[32] Relying increasingly on his own judgment, especially in regard to American art, Corcoran's collecting expanded to include sculpture.

As in the case of William Walters, Corcoran's collection was initially contained in his home. By 1851, arrangements had been made for twice weekly public viewings;[33] however, opening the doors to his home did not suffice. Unlike other contemporary American collectors, Corcoran was determined to place his collection in a building "expressly designed and constructed as a great gallery."[34] Construction of a gallery, designed by John Renwick, was begun in 1859 and completed twelve years later, in 1871. The collection was formally presented to the public in 1874.[35] The singularity of his approach was further underlined in 1869, when Corcoran transferred the deed of the Gallery to a Board of Trustees, which was charged with the supervision of the building's completion and the accommodation of Corcoran's collection. Corcoran also provided acquisition and maintenance funds, and transmitted "assurances from friends in other cities . . . that they will contribute fine works of art from their respective collections."[36] Corcoran viewed the Gallery as a necessary addition to the nation's capital.[37] His contemporaries further recognized it as an instrument for "awakening that taste for art which Mr. Corcoran is so anxious to cultivate in his countrymen."[38]

Corcoran had an agenda even more distinctly different from that of other collectors. He was concerned not only with the aesthetic development of the citizenry but also with the encouragement and assistance of artists. Indeed, Corcoran intended the Gallery to be more than

a mere exhibition of fine pictures and sculpture, but a lyceum where scholars may come to study the achievements of the masters and where the people may come to hear from learned lips the precious lessons of experience. In the Louvre, and the other grand galleries of Europe, youth of both sexes come to take copies from the rare originals; and it may be that in the course of time, the Corcoran Gallery will be equally crowded with candidates for superiority in these same high aspirations.[39]

It is in the context of Corcoran's broad goals of educating the public, training young artists, and providing an arena for contemporary art that the commission of the Barye bronzes in 1873 must be considered. With his interest in American art, Corcoran encouraged the acquisitions committee to obtain representative examples of contemporary native artists. The Gallery's interests were not parochial, however, as is evident from Walters' purchases.[40] The need to incorporate important examples of contemporary European art was consistent with Corcoran's pedagogical goals for the institution.

One hundred twenty Barye bronzes were ordered

through Lucas for the Corcoran Gallery.[41] By 1875, one hundred seven pieces had been received and installed with the assistance of Walters in the library of the newly opened Corcoran Gallery.[42] Their placement should not be viewed as either a degradation of sculpture in general or of the bronzes in particular. On the contrary, it should be noted that Corcoran's single greatest expenditure had been for Hiram Powers' *Greek Slave*. Not only was this sculpture considered the prize of the collection and prominently displayed in the Octagon Room, but the sculpture gallery itself was allotted dominant and considerable space.[43] The placement of Barye's generally small bronze pieces was consistent with the practice of contemporary European collectors. It might also be suggested that this was actually an acknowledgment of their singularity and the requirement of a special environment for their display.

The bronzes were executed under the direct supervision of Barye. Since his concern with the quality of production had always been an essential feature of his artistic temperament, it must have played a particularly significant role in reference to the Corcoran project. This must have been especially true since the commission represented a level of recognition the sculptor had not previously experienced. Barye testified to this when he reflected, "My own country has not done this for me."[44]

Whether through individual and independent or cooperative and organized acquisitions, Barye's work was broadly acknowledged in the last quarter of the nineteenth century. His international audience included connoisseurs, critics, artists, students, and the general public. The acceptance of a sculptural genre once viewed as revolutionary was complete.

## NOTES

1  See Saint-Chéron, "De la Dècadence de l'Ecole des Beaux-Arts," *L'Artiste*, 1st ser., VIII (1834), 108–109.

2  During the Second Empire, the established rate was 2,400 francs for busts and 8,000 to 15,000 francs for statues. Thérèse Burollet, "Le Command," in *The Second Empire, 1852–1870: Art in France Under Napoleon III* (Philadelphia, 1978), 225.

3  Veronique Wiesinger, "Le Concours," in *La Sculpture Française au XIX<sup>e</sup> Siècle* (Paris, 1986), 216.

4  For a discussion of the system, see Chantal Martinet, "La Souscription," in *La Sculpture Française*, 231–38.

5  The public's favorite artists included Thomas Couture, Alexandre Cabanel, Louis Boulanger, Léon Cogniet, Eugène Delacroix, Jean-Léon Gérôme, Jean-Louis Ernest Meissonier, Louis-Gabriel-Eugène Isabey, Théodore Rousseau, Jean-Baptiste Carpeaux, and Frédéric Auguste Bartholdi. Jean-Marie Moulin, "The Second Empire: Art and Society," in *The Second Empire*, 12.

6  For a discussion and illustrations of interiors, see "Furnishings," in *The Second Empire*, 74–82.

7  *Ibid.*, 82.

8  For a discussion of French taste and collecting, see *ibid.*, 11–28, 35–359.

9  "Barye," *Art Journal*, 50 (1880), 21.

10  This has been attributed to the persistance of doubts about the legitimacy of animal sculptures as well as uncertainty about the quality of the casting. It should be recalled that Barye had temporarily

relinquished ownership of the models and was unable to control production. See the correspondence of both George Lucas (in the archives of the Baltimore Museum of Art) and Cyrus Lawrence (in the archives of the Museum of Fine Arts, Boston).

11  "Barye," *Art Journal*, 24.

12  It has been suggested that despite English audiences' admiration of realism, Barye's highly charged and almost cruelly honest representations may have appeared extreme to them. Jane Horswell, *Bronze Sculpture of 'Les Animaliers': Reference and Price Guide* (Clopton, England, 1971), 4. The French animaliers who were popular in England were inevitably those who dealt with domesticated animals and familiar hunt and racing scenes, typically defined by a combination of realism and sentimentality.

13  Rose V. S. Berry, "William Morris Hunt: American Painters Who Have Especially Influenced American Art," *Art and Archaeology*, 15, no. 5 (May 1923), 207.

14  For a detailed analysis of Lucas' position vis-à-vis American collecting and for supporting documentation from his diaries, see Lillian M. C. Randall, *The Diary of George Lucas: An American Art Agent in Paris, 1857–1909* (2 vols; Princeton, 1979).

15  *Ibid.*

16  For a discussion of Frick's role in collecting and his relationship to Lucas, see Lillian M. C. Randall, "An American Abroad: Visits to Sculptors' Studios in the 1860's," *The Journal of the Walters Art Gallery*, 33–34, (1970–1971), 42–51.

17  Prices for Barye's works ranged from 50 to 150 francs, compared

to, for example, Schneck's rural genre scenes, which sold for 500 to 1,000 francs. See Lucas entries in Randall, *The Diary of George Lucas*, 146, 166–67.

18 Part of the appeal of collecting was affordability. Lucas' entries, however, testify to a steady increase in prices. By 1884, the purchase price for a Barye seated lion was 8,500 francs. During the same period, Lucas paid 10,000 francs for Millet's *Sower*. See Lucas' entries, *ibid.*, 586, and Randall's commentaries, *ibid.*, 25.

19 See Randall's commentaries on Lucas, *ibid.*, 12–13.

20 *Ibid.*, 25.

21 Lucas' own extensive Barye collection is now in the Baltimore Museum of Art.

22 Randall, *The Diary of George Lucas*, 4.

23 William R. Johnston, "The Barye Collection of the Walters Art Gallery, Baltimore," *Apollo*, 50 (November 1974), 402.

24 Randall, *The Diary of George Lucas*, 13.

25 Correspondence in the Baltimore Museum of Art chronicles the extensive and detailed exchange between Lucas and Walters regarding purchases.

26 Johnston, "The Barye Collection," 402, 406.

27 William Thompson Walters, comp., *Antoine-Louis Barye from the French of Various Critics* (Baltimore, 1885), 5.

28 *Ibid.*, 6.

29 M. E. P. Bouligny, *A Tribute to W. W. Corcoran of Washington City* (Philadelphia, 1874), 39–40.

30 *Ibid.*, 8–18. These included generous support of orphanages and a home for impoverished women; assistance in the establishment of the Smithsonian Institution and the Mechanics Institute; and sizable gifts to William and Mary College, the University of Virginia, and Columbia College.

31 *Corcoran* (Washington, D.C., 1976), 12–13.

32 For a listing and description of individual works in the collection, see Bouligny, *A Tribute to W. W. Corcoran*, 45–81.

33 *Corcoran*, 47.

34 *A Grandfather's Legacy: Containing a Sketch of His Life* (Washington, D.C., 1879), 535.

35 Completion was delayed by the Civil War and the government's appropriation of the building. It should be noted that in 1897 a new building was constructed. Today, the original Corcoran building is the Renwick Gallery, a part of the National Museum of American Art.

36 *A Grandfather's Legacy*, 32.

37 *Ibid.*, 33.

38 *Ibid.*, 536.

39 *Ibid.*, 136.

40 In 1874, three-quarters of the collection consisted of European pieces.

41 While the most complete collections of Barye bronzes are in the Walters Art Gallery, the Baltimore Museum of Art, and the Corcoran Gallery of Art, substantial collections are also contained in the Metropolitan Museum of Art, the Brooklyn Musem of Art, the Philadelphia Museum of Art, the Fogg Art Museum, and the Museum of Fine Arts, Boston.

42 Randall, *The Diary of George Lucas*, 14.

43 Bouligny, *A Tribute to W. W. Corcoran*, 39.

44 Walters, *Barye*, 6.

# TECHNICAL EXAMINATION OF

# THE BARYE BRONZES

Meg Loew Craft

The collection of bronzes by Barye at the Corcoran Gallery of Art is unique in that it was ordered as a group from Barye's atelier. William T. Walters, a board member whose own collection of Barye bronzes became a centerpiece of the Walters Art Gallery in Baltimore, bought the works on the Corcoran's behalf. Purchased in 1873, two years before Barye's death, all the bronzes, as far as can be determined, appear in his last catalogue, *Quai des Celestins 4*, published in 1865. The collection is important not only artistically but also for study and research purposes, because many of Barye's sculptures were cast with or without his permission both during his lifetime and posthumously. Since casting is a mechanical, repetitive process and not a creative act, recognizing and attributing Barye's authorized bronzes without documentary evidence has proved to be a virtually impossible task.

Although technical examinations of the bronzes have been limited in the past, those conducted have revealed interesting details of Barye's working habits. Unfortunately, the information acquired does not help to characterize Barye's work. Instead, it reinforces the conclusion that historic documentation is necessary and that documented collections, such as that of the Corcoran, are important to understand the artist and his methods.

## Casting

Bronze sculpture can be cast by two basic methods: sand casting or *cire perdue* (lost-wax casting). From ancient times to the nineteenth century, lost-wax casting was practiced almost exclusively. With the increased collecting of decorative art sculpture in the 1800s, sand casting replaced lost-wax casting as the preferred method of production. Sand casting simplified and quickened the process of reproducing sculptures and, as a result, reduced the cost. Not entirely abandoned, the lost-wax method was reserved by Barye for the production of the most important and singular of commissions, such as the monumental *Lion Crushing a Serpent*, now in the Louvre. Despite the fact that an artist's sculptural detail is carried through to the final work more precisely in the lost-wax method, all the bronzes by Barye in the Corcoran's collection, from the evidence available, appear to have been made by the sand-casting method.

The initial step of either casting method is the making of the artist's original sculpture into a workable medium, usually wax or clay. Both are readily modeled, but they are structurally weak and often require a supporting armature of wire or wood. To further increase the workability of the wax, materials such as honey or molasses can be added to the medium.

When multiple copies are to be made by sand casting, the next step is to produce a plaster mold, or negative, of the object that can be used to form the maquette, a copy in plaster that is stronger than the original version. The inherently weak initial sculpture may be damaged or destroyed in the process of creating the mold. In addition, the maquette may be scored with incised grids or other markings that are used as guides in the reproduction process.

According to Barye's procedure for sand casting, after the plaster mold and maquette are made, a bronze model is produced and used in the making of sand molds for edition casts. Great attention is paid to the finishing, or cold-working, of the bronze model, for the detail of this model transfers to all the edition casts. Such intentional models can generally be distinguished from edition casts in several ways: thin patinas may be abraded by the molding sand; joins between individual sections of the object may be only coarsely pinned together or may detach completely; and the surfaces will be extensively cold-worked or finished.

To produce a mold, damp, fine grained sand is tamped into a flask, one half of a topless and bottomless retaining form of iron that is large enough to contain the object. Surfaces of the sand and the object are dusted with a separating agent, usually talcum, flour, or chalk, to prevent sticking. Once half of the object is pressed into the sand, a second, open, keyed flask is secured on top. Sand is then tamped into the second flask to bury the remaining, exposed half of the object. In making a sand mold of complicated forms, undercuts are individually filled with separate sections of sand that can be easily removed to prevent damaging the mold. After the flasks are carefully separated, the model is removed. For the sake of economy and technique requirements, castings are usually hollow. Next, a core, a rough shape slightly smaller than the actual model, is made of sand or clay and is fixed floating inside the negative sand mold with thin pins. The space or gap between the core and the walls of the sand mold will eventually be filled with the molten bronze, which results in a hollow casting.

After the model is removed and the core prepared, channels are impressed or cut into the sand to allow the metal to be poured in and the gases and fumes to escape during casting. A large channel, or sprue, cut through or impressed into the sand from the edge of the flask to the void created by the model allows the molten bronze to fill the empty space. Vents, smaller channels, or cuts strategically placed around the faces of the sand mold allow air and the gases formed during casting to escape from the space to be filled with bronze. After all the channels are cut and the core is inserted, the flasks are clamped together again.

The mold is now ready for the molten copper alloy to be poured in. After the metal is poured and the casting cooled, the flask is disassembled and the casting removed. All the flaws remaining from the casting procedure are removed during the finishing process. These flaws include excess metal that enters the vents or sprues during pouring, fins of metal that seep between the sections of the sand mold, holes produced by trapped gases or where metal is unable to flow, and cracks caused by shrinkage during cooling. The core is usually removed. During casting the surface of the core sand becomes burned black and grey. Traces of burned

Fig. 77. Detail of *Ocelot Carrying Off a Heron* (73.66). (1) Burned sand, (2) core pins, and (3) fins from between mold sections remain after the casting process.

Fig. 78. Detail of *Fawn Reclining* (74.32). Cast surface without cold-working.

Fig. 79. Detail of *Fawn Scratching* (68.14). Cast surface extensively cold-worked.

sand, core pins, and fins located between mold sections are visible on many of the bronzes, especially on the less finished interior areas (fig. 77).

In the finishing steps, casting features, such as fins, are first removed and flaws are repaired. Next, the surface is filed, polished, and cold-worked as desired. While the slightly granular texture from the sand that usually remains on the cast surface can be diminished with polishing, the surface is often left as is on edition casts (fig. 78). Generally, however, the finer the cast, the more extensive the finishing will be. Details of design can be added, intensified, or altered during chiselling or cold-working (fig. 79). Tool marks and sharp-edged incisions indicate cold-working after casting. Barye added his personal stamp and number during this step of production.

Sand casting does not transfer the detail on the model as clearly and crisply to the cast as does lost-wax casting. When multiples are made in lost-wax casting, the waxes can be individually worked before they are cast to insure crisp detail. Although the sand mold can be reused many times, it progressively looses detail and definition, and it cannot be modified once it is made. Also, the later in the edition the casting is made, the poorer the quality of its cast-through detail. On edition casts, the signature and some significant details are often reinforced by cold-working (fig. 80).

The final step is patination, in which chemicals are applied with heat to the finished surface of the casting and rubbed to produce a range of colors. Enormous variety is possible not only from object to object but also on the same object by using different chemicals, multiple applications, and by varying the thickness of layers of patinating chemicals. Two chemicals dominating the patinas in the Corcoran's collection are copper sulfate, which produces a green color, and liver of sulfur, which produces black.

## Technical Examination

Beyond being purchased at the same time, these bronzes also have similar features resulting from the manufacturing process. Based on visual examination of accessible surfaces, the bronzes appear to be sand cast. No indication of the use of *cire perdue* (lost-wax casting), direct or indirect method, is apparent. It is unlikely that inaccessible surfaces contain evidence to the contrary. The sculptures are all edition casts; no models appear to be included in the collection.

Typically, the detail on the sculpture is cast through from the model with minimal cold-working beyond the removal of the evidence of manufacturing, such as the pins supporting the core, the pouring gates and vents, and the fins between sections of the sand mold. Even though the detail is readable, it is not as detailed and crisp as on corresponding bronze models. The patination of many Barye bronzes varies greatly, but here the majority of the castings were first painted green before an upper black layer of varying thickness was applied. In the end, the opacity and continuous nature of this black layer determine whether the object appears black with green highlights (or vice versa), dark green, or black.

Barye typically marked his castings in two ways: by printing "Barye" or "A. L. Barye" into the clay or wax base of the original sculpture; or by inscribing "Barye" into the bronze after casting and before patination (fig. 81). Frequently, the signature that carried through from the model was shallow or faint and had to be reinforced by cold-working during finishing. A date sometimes seen with the signature is when the casting was first issued or the model was made, not the casting date of a specific object (fig. 82).

A small, rectangular steel stamp bearing "Barye" in blocklike capital letters was also used to mark some of the works. Barye applied this stamp during the finishing operations and before patination. The presence of the stamp has been taken as an indication that Barye was personally involved in the supervision or production of that individual casting.[1] During the period Barye operated his own foundry, many of the castings were marked with the stamp and followed by a number, which indicated a cast's position within an edition. Stamping each sculpture was only done on a regular basis for a brief period of time since the foundry was not financially successful. For a period after the failure of his foundry, Barye lost possession of his dies and some models.[2] In later years, Barye used the stamp sporadically on works such as the *Card Receiver with Fawn's Feet* (74.45; fig. 83).

Once a model or even an edition casting entered

Fig. 80. Detail of *Python Crushing a Gazelle* (73.87). The "A. L." appears as cast through from the model while "Barye" has been reinforced after casting.

Fig. 81. Detail of *Card Receiver* (74.46). Signature incised after casting.

Fig. 82. Detail of *Lion Devouring a Doe* (73.47). Signature and date cast through from the model.

Fig. 83. Detail of *Card Receiver with Fawn's Feet* (74.45). Personal stamp applied to bronze after casting.

Fig. 84. Detail of *Virginia Deer* (74.44). Personal stamp and number cast through from the model.

Fig. 85. Detail of *Lion Devouring a Doe* (73.47). Oval paper label bearing the handwritten last catalogue number and the black "2" found on the underside of the bases in the Corcoran collection.

another foundry, copies could be made without Barye's permission or involvement. Since signatures and stamps were cast through from the model, copies also bear Barye's name. During the time when the dies were out of Barye's possession, the original stamps also may have been used to mark casts.

The Corcoran's collection contains examples both of Barye's signature cast through from the model and of his personal stamp. Two sculptures and a plaque—*Fawn Reclining* (74.32), *Lion Devouring a Doe* (73.47), and *Virginia Deer* (relief, 74.44)—bear Barye's personal stamp cast through from a model (fig. 84). The presence of the personal stamp indicates that Barye either stamped some of his models or permitted existing stamped edition casts to be used as models. In any case, it is clear that Barye did not exclusively apply the stamp during

finishing. Only one casting owned by the Corcoran, the brown, patinated *Card Receiver with Fawn's Feet* (74.45), has the personal stamp directly impressed during the cold-working process; no number accompanies this stamp.

In addition to the manufacturing features, other markings are present on the Corcoran's bronzes. Since the origin is unknown, they or similar markings may appear on other authorized Barye castings. Many of the castings have attached to the underside of the base an old, gummed paper sticker, oval with a blue printed border, bearing the *Quai des Celestins* catalogue number handwritten in an acidic sepia-toned ink. The labels may have been applied in Barye's atelier or soon after the works were acquired by the Corcoran. While a few of the labels are legible, many are fragmentary or remain only as shadows on the underside of the base, where the label's adhesive disturbed the patina. A large "2" was also added in black paint on the underside of the base on most of the castings. Like the paper labels, only the shadow of this number, where the patination is disturbed, remains on many castings (fig. 85).

A superb craftsman, Barye was noted for the high quality of his castings. He also stated in his writings that an alloy of 90% copper and 10% tin, known as "Barye's bronze," be used to cast sculptures to be finished in his atelier.[3] Other additives, such as lead and zinc, were regularly added to make the metal flow more easily, to melt at lower temperatures, and to improve the quality of the casting. No past analysis of Barye bronzes is available.

Three sculptures were selected for analysis. *Two Young Lions* (73.46) was chosen because the casting exhibited extensive cold-working and variety in patination, and it was sand cast in a single piece. *Python Crushing a Gazelle* (73.87), a sculpture sand cast in many separate sections and joined, was also picked. Its patina, black over a green layer, typifies most of the castings in the Corcoran's collection. Additionally, its sculptural detail was primarily cast through from the model with very little cold-working. The third documented casting analyzed was *Ape Riding a Gnu* (73.40), which was probably sand cast in a traditional manner. The base and the extremities of the ape and gnu were cast separately and joined, as were many of Barye's figurative sculptures.

For comparison, two other of Barye's bronzes, not part of the initial purchase, were also examined by quantitative x-ray fluorescence analysis. Both bronzes have Barye's signature cast through from the model, considerable cold-working, and variegated patinas. Compared to the group purchased in 1873, the quality of the casts is good. *Pointer* (68.15) was issued in authorized editions by Barye and proportedly edited posthumously by La Fontaine. *Fawn Scratching* (68.14), a subject modeled by Barye but never produced in his lifetime, was cast posthumously by Ingliss.[4]

In selecting these five castings, several questions were

investigated. Did Barye frequently use an alloy close to 90:10 bronze? Could the documented Barye castings be distinguished by composition from the two castings he probably did not authorize? Could separately cast sections of a sculpture be distinguished from one another?

Although an extensive study was not undertaken, several castings were analyzed by Mrs. Janice Carlson of the Scientific Research Laboratory at the Henry Francis du Pont Winterthur Museum in Winterthur, Delaware. To produce the data listed below, two parts of each of the following objects were examined by quantitative energy dispersive x-ray fluorescence analysis.

| Object | Part | Cu | Zn | Sn | Pb | Sb | Ag | Fe |
|---|---|---|---|---|---|---|---|---|
| *Pointer* | Side | 83.39 | 7.62 | 5.39 | 3.22 | 0.07 | 0.15 | 0.13 |
| 68.15 | Base | 82.48 | 9.08 | 4.88 | 3.30 | 0.03 | 0.11 | 0.11 |
| *Fawn* | Side | 90.26 | 7.25 | 1.97 | 0.40 | 0.02 | 0.04 | 0.08 |
| 68.14 | Base | 76.58 | 7.00 | 15.40 | 0.14 | 0.28 | 0.33 | 0.22 |
| *Ape/Gnu* | Side | 86.92 | 4.35 | 6.84 | 1.45 | 0.11 | 0.13 | 0.15 |
| 73.40 | Base | 88.37 | 5.63 | 4.16 | 1.63 | 0.06 | 0.07 | 0.08 |
| *Python* | Side | 84.77 | 5.97 | 6.18 | 2.66 | 0.06 | 0.08 | 0.24 |
| 73.87 | Base | 83.42 | 5.90 | 5.54 | 4.73 | 0.07 | 0.08 | 0.25 |
| *Two Lions* | Side | 91.65 | 4.11 | 3.64 | 0.30 | 0.06 | 0.06 | 0.17 |
| 73.46 | Base | 91.43 | 3.88 | 3.83 | 0.64 | 0.08 | 0.05 | 0.07 |

Analysis revealed that Barye did not use the 90% copper/10% tin alloy for any of the three casts from the Corcoran's original purchase. The documented Barye bronzes, the unprovenanced *Pointer*, and the posthumously cast *Fawn Scratching* were all made of more common alloys containing intentional additions of lead and zinc.

Bronze is a copper alloy with a greater content of tin than zinc. Brass, also a copper alloy, contains more zinc than tin. *Fawn Scratching* varied significantly from the other castings in composition, revealing higher amounts of tin in the base and zinc in the figure of the deer. The deer itself appears to be composed of the copper and zinc alloy of brass rather than of bronze. Based on the analysis it can be safely stated that the base and the deer were cast separately and then joined. The interior of the casting could not be examined since the bronze cannot be removed from its red marble base. *Pointer* has a slightly higher zinc content in both the dog and the base.

Considerable variation in composition was found from object to object as well as from area to area on the same object. If the 90% copper/10% tin alloy was in fact used, perhaps it was employed only in a few of Barye's most unique or experimental sculptures.

## NOTES

I wish to thank Mrs. Janice Carlson and Dr. George Reilly of the Henry Francis du Pont Winterthur Museum in Winterthur, Delaware, for analyzing the five sculptures.

1 Jeanne L. Wasserman, *Sculpture by Antoine-Louis Barye in the Collection of the Fogg Art Museum* (Cambridge, MA, 1982), 12.

2 Stuart Pivar, *The Barye Bronzes: A Catalogue Raisonné* (Woodbridge, Suffolk, 1974), 24.

3 *Ibid.*, 26.

4 *Ibid.*, 39, 43.

## Notes on the Catalogue

This catalogue is arranged according to subject following the general divisions in Stuart Pivar's *The Barye Bronzes*. Groups with human forms appear in the first category of *Figures*. *Animals* come next and are listed alphabetically; single animals precede groups. All animals of the deer family appear together. The last category is *Decorative Arts*. *Watercolors* are listed separately at the end.

Measurements of sculptures are maximum dimensions, given in inches and (centimeters), height preceding length and depth. Except when noted, measurements include base. For watercolors, height precedes width.

The location of Barye's signature on the bronzes is often designated PR or PL, meaning proper right or left of the animal depicted. These abbreviations sometimes appear in other parts of an entry.

Several terms under the head "casting" require explanation. "Separate base" is used only when the base has been cast by itself without any major compositional elements and is mechanically fastened to the body of the piece. All pieces by necessity have had cold-working to remove casting features (fins, seams, pins, etc.). The term, when used here, means that further work enhanced or added detail to the sculpture.

Titles are given in both English and French. An asterisk before the title indicates that the work is included in the exhibition. Many of the bronzes have been known by several different titles in the past. I have followed, for the most part, Pivar, who uses the French titles that appear in Barye's final catalogue of 1865, from which the Corcoran pieces were ordered. Pivar's English titles are, in general, direct translations of the French. In a few cases, I have used other traditional English titles, for example, *Lion Crushing a Serpent* instead of *Lion and Serpent*, when I feel they more accurately reflect the meaning of the French or are more informative. Occasionally, particularly with deer subjects, there remains some doubt as to the actual

piece listed in Barye's 1865 catalogue. In those instances, I have kept the title given in early catalogues of the Corcoran collection, which appear to be based on purchase records. Whenever this has been done, the title is followed by (?). Under the head "literature," I have noted significant variations of the title as given by Pivar or by Glenn F. Benge in his catalogue raisonné of *The Sculpture of Antoine-Louis Barye in American Collections*.

Dating of specific castings is problematic since Barye undoubtedly produced casts of individual works for many years after they were first modeled. Approximate dates, in general, are those proposed by Benge in his catalogue raisonné. A specific date following the phrase "Salon of" refers to when a work was first exhibited at the Salon. In some instances, two dates are given: the first is usually from Benge; the date in parentheses is taken from early Corcoran catalogues of the Barye collection. When a date appearing only in Pivar is used, it is followed by a "P." Works designated "new models" in Barye's 1865 catalogue have dates in brackets; the first date refers to Barye's previous catalogue. These late dates are used even when the work, such as *Peasant of the Middle Ages*, was part of an earlier group. Other specific dates or ranges of dates are based on Barye's catalogues or other external evidence.

Citations under literature ("lit.") refer to the catalogue raisonnés of the bronzes by Pivar and Benge; the catalogue of the Fogg Collection by Wasserman; and the catalogue raisonné of watercolors by Zieseniss. The Pivar and Benge numbers generally refer to a subject, not to the specific piece in the Corcoran collection. Benge, however, usually notes the Corcoran example, which is indicated by a letter following the number.

Technical information on patination, casting, and condition as well as measurements and location of signature were supplied by Meg Loew Craft. Dare Hartwell, the Corcoran's conservator, assisted Ms. Craft in the gathering and checking of this information. EJN

Fig. 86. *Tartar Warrior Checking His Horse.*

# CATALOGUE

## Figures

**\*General Bonaparte** (1838)
*Le général Bonaparte*

signed: BARYE cast on PR rear top corner of
base
size: H. 13″ (33.0cm); L. 10¼″ (26.0cm);
D. 4¾″ (12.0cm)
patination: red-brown with thin green
highlights on horse; blackish highlights on
base
casting: sand; at least 31 pieces, including
separate base; extensive filing
condition: patina damaged
lit.: Benge, 206a; Pivar, F1
73.26
Fig. 58

**\*Caucasian Warrior** [1855–65]
*Guerrier du Caucase*

signed: BARYE cast on rear PR corner of base
size: H. 7⅝″ (19.3cm); L. 7⅛″ (18.0cm);
D. 3⅛″ (8.0cm)
patination: heavy, opaque black over green
casting: sand probably; at least 10 pieces,
including separate base
condition: losses in patina on warrior,
especially back
lit.: Benge, 202a; Pivar, F24
73.91
Fig. 64

**\*Charles VII Victorious** (1839)
*Charles VII, le Victorieux*

signed: BARYE cast and reinforced on top PL
side of base
size: H. 11¾″ (29.8cm); L. 10⅜″ (26.4cm);
D. 4¼″ (10.8cm)
patination: black over green
casting: sand; 17 major but 25 overall pieces,
including separate base
condition: sword bent
lit.: Benge, 203d; Pivar, F8
73.30
Fig. 59

**\*Duke of Orléans** (1840)
*Le Duc d'Orléans*

signed: BARYE cast and reinforced by incising
on PR rear corner of base
size: H. 14⅜″ (36.5cm); L. 12⅝″ (32.0cm);
D. 5⅛″ (13.0cm)
patination: black over green

casting: sand; more than 22 pieces, including
separate base
condition: blade of scabbard missing; extensive
losses in patina
lit.: Benge, 204a; Pivar, F5
73.27
Fig. 61

**\*Equestrienne in 1830 Dress** ca. 1840
*Amazone, costume de 1830*

signed: BARYE cast and reinforced by incising
on PL top side of base
size: H. 15″ (38.0cm); L. 13⅞″ (35.3 cm);
D. 4⅝″ (11.9cm)
patination: black over green
casting: sand; at least 17 pieces, including
separate base
condition: riding crop missing; overall losses in
patina; patina overpainted on horse's back
near tail
lit.: Benge, 200b; Pivar, F6
73.28
Fig. 62

**\*Huntsman, Louis XV Period** [1855–65]
*Piqueur, costume Louis XV*

signed: BARYE cast on top PR rear corner of
base
size: H. 7⅝″ (19.3cm); L. 7½″ (19.0cm); D. 3″
(7.5cm)
patination: heavy, opaque black over green
casting: sand probably; at least 14 pieces,
including separate base
condition: losses in patina
lit.: Benge, 208; Pivar, F23
73.90
Fig. 63

**\*Indian Mounted on an Elephant Crushing a
Tiger** late 1830s
*Indien monté sur un éléphant écrasant un tigre*

signed: BARYE cast on PL corner of base
size: H. 11″ (27.6cm); L. 12⅛″ (30.9cm); D. 7″
(17.9cm)
patination: opaque black over green
casting: sand; at least 8 pieces
condition: patina worn in high points; base
dented
lit.: Benge, 183c; Pivar, F14
73.34
Fig. 21

**\*Juno** before 1847
*Junon*

signed: BARYE incised on base PL side of front
size: H. 12¼″ (31.1cm); L. 5⅛″ (13.0cm);
D. 5⅞″ (14.8cm)
patination: black over green
casting: sand; at least 8 pieces
condition: patina abraded on thighs and base;
staff bent
lit.: Benge, 230l; Pivar, F19
73.37
Fig. 53

**\*Minerva** before 1847
*Minerve*

signed: BARYE incised on front PR of base
size: H. 12¼″ (31.2cm); L. 5⅛″ (13.0cm);
D. 6⅜″ (16.3cm)
patination: black over green
casting: sand; at least 11 pieces, including
separate base
condition: some losses in patina
lit.: Benge, 230p; Pivar, F18
73.36
Fig. 52

**\*North African Horseman Surprised by a
Serpent** ca. 1835–37
*Cavalier africain surpris par un serpent*

signed: BARYE cast on PR end of base
size: H. 8⅞″ (22.5cm); L. 11¼″ (28.6cm);
D. 7⅛″ (18.0cm)
patination: brown with green and black
highlights
casting: sand; at least 16 pieces; cold-working
condition: weapon in PR hand missing
lit.: Benge, 193; Pivar, F13
73.33
Fig. 25

**\*Peasant of the Middle Ages** [1855–65]
*Paysan du moyen âge*

signed: BARYE cast on top center front of base
size: H. 13″ (33.0cm); L. 10½″ (26.8cm);
D. 4½″ (11.5cm)
patination: black over green
casting: sand; at least 11 pieces, including
separate base
condition: feather repaired
lit.: Benge, 168e; Pivar, F25; Fogg, 30
74.23
Fig. 57

**\*Roger and Angelica on the Hippogriff**
ca. 1840 (1846)
*Angélique et Roger montés sur l'hippogriffe*

signed: BARYE inscribed on PL side top of
base near octopus
size: H. 20⅜″ (51.8cm); L. 23⅛″ (58.8cm);
D. 11½″ (29.2cm)
patination: black over green
casting: sand; over 30 pieces
condition: top of scabbard bent and missing;
tip of PR wing bent; patina worn on high
points
lit.: Benge, 222c; Pivar, F16
73.35
Fig. 50

**\*Tartar Warrior Checking His Horse** 1830s
*Guerrier tartare arrêtant son cheval*

signed: BARYE cast and reinforced on top PR
 front of base
size: H. 12¾″ (32.3cm); L. 13⅜″ (34.0cm);
 D. 5⅞″ (15.0cm)
pedestal: H. 6⅛″ (15.5cm); L. 17⅜″ (44.0cm);
 D. 10⅝″ (27.0cm)
patination: black over green
casting: sand; at least 30 pieces, not including
 pedestal; pedestal sand cast separately in
 many pieces
condition: plume finial on helmet missing
lit.: Benge, 209e; Pivar, F9
73.31
Fig. 86

**\*Lapith (Theseus) Fighting a Centaur**
 (sketch) ca. 1840
*Lapithe et Centaure; Thésée combattant le centaure
Biénor, esquisse*

signed: BARYE incised on base beneath PR
 rear leg
size: H. 13½″ (34.3cm); L. 14⅜″ (36.5cm);
 D. 5½″ (14.0cm)
patination: black over green
casting: sand; at least 12 pieces, including
 separate base
condition: losses of patina above PR clavicle,
 neck, rear legs, and other high points
lit.: Benge, 218d; Pivar, F22
73.39
Fig. 48

**\*Theseus Fighting the Centaur Biénor**
 Salon of 1850–51
*Thésée combattant le centaure Biénor*

signed: A.L. Barye/Paris 1850, cast on PL rear
 side of base
size: H. 44½″ (113.0cm); L. 49⅝″ (126.0cm);
 D. 16″ (40.5cm)
patination: green over black
casting: sand probably; more than 30 pieces;
 carefully finished
lit.: Benge, 223; Pivar, F21
74.68
Figs. 5, 47

**\*Theseus Fighting the Minotaur** ca. 1843
*Thésée combattant le minotaure*

signed: BARYE incised on top of base, PL side
size: H. 17¾″ (45.0cm); L. 11¾″ (29.8cm);
 D. 6⅜″ (16.1cm)
patination: black over green
casting: sand; at least 19 pieces, including
 separate base; minor cold-working
condition: blade of sword replaced
lit.: Benge, 225d; Pivar, F20
73.38
Fig. 45

**\*Two Arab Horsemen Killing a Lion**
 late 1830s
*Deux cavaliers arabes tuant un lion*

signed: BARYE cast and reinforced on top of
 base, PL rear corner
size: H. 14⅛″ (36.0cm); L. 14⅞″ (37.7cm);
 D. 9″ (23.0cm)
patination: black over green
casting: sand; approximately 32 pieces
lit.: Benge, 188c; Pivar, F10
73.32
Fig. 23

# Animals

## Ape

**\*Ape Riding a Gnu** ca. 1845 [1842P]
*Singe monté sur un gnou*

signed: BARYE cast center front of base
size: H. 9¼″ (23.5cm); L. 10⅜″ (26.5cm);
 D. 4″ (10.0cm)
patination: green with overlying brown
 highlights
casting: sand; at least 7 pieces; extensive cold-
 working; analyzed by the Scientific Research
 Lab, Winterthur Museum
lit.: Benge, 201c; Pivar, A1
73.40

## Basset

**\*English Basset** 1830s
*Basset anglais*

signed: BARYE cast on top of base
size: H. 6¼″ (15.9cm); L. 8¾″ (22.3cm);
 D. 3⅝″ (9.3cm)
patination: very heavy opaque black over
 green
casting: sand; 1 piece; tail filed
condition: base abraded; patina missing from
 center of base
lit.: Benge, 2d (as *Standing Basset*); Pivar, A27
73.44
Fig. 17

## Bear

**\*Seated Bear** 1830s [Salon of 1837?]
*Ours assis*

signed: BARYE incised on base at bear's back
size: H. 5½″ (14.0cm); L. 8″ (20.4cm); D. 5¾″
 (14.5cm)
patination: brown with traces of green and
 black
casting: sand; 1 piece
lit.: Benge, 4d; Pivar, A5
73.43
Fig. 12

**\*Standing Bear** Salon of 1831
*Ours debout*

signed: BARYE incised on front of base
size: H. 9⅝″ (24.4cm); L. 4½″ (11.5cm);
 D. 3¾″ (9.7cm)
patination: thin, transparent black over green
casting: sand; 1 piece
condition: core and armature in situ
lit.: Benge, 5d; Pivar, A3
73.41
Fig. 19

**\*Bear Fleeing from Dogs** [1855–65]
*Ours fuyant les chiens*

signed: BARYE probably cast, reinforced by
 incising, PL side of base below bear's head
size: H. 14″ (35.7cm); L. 17¾″ (45.0cm);
 D. 10″ (25.4cm)
patination: very thin black over green;
 appearance is green
casting: sand; at least 28 pieces, including
 separate base; minor cold-working
condition: bronze exposed on worn high
 points
lit.: Benge, 168b; Pivar, A8
73.93
Fig. 26

**\*Bear Overthrown by Hounds** [1855–65]
*Ours terrassé par des chiens de grande race*

signed: BARYE incised top of base under dog
 attacking bear's stomach
size: H. 10⅛″ (25.6cm); L. 13⅝″ (34.5cm);
 D. 10⅜″ (26.5cm)
patination: black over green
casting: sand; at least 5 pieces, including
 separate base; each animal appears to be
 cast as one piece
condition: patina worn on high points
lit.: Benge, 176a; Pivar, A7
73.92

**\*Two Bears Fighting** Salon of 1833
*Lutte de deux ours; Groupe d'ours*

signed: BARYE cast on front of base
size: H. 8¼″ (21.0cm); L. 6¼″ (16.0cm);
 D. 5½″ (14.0cm)
patination: black over green
casting: sand; 2 pieces
lit.: Benge, 110c; Pivar, A4
73.42

**Bull**

**\*Bull** 1830s (1841)
*Taureau*

signed: BARYE cast, top of base by PR front
 leg
size: H. 7¼″ (18.5cm); L. 11⅞″ (30.3cm);
 D. 4¼″ (10.7cm)
patination: black over green
casting: sand; at least 2 pieces (bull and base)
lit.: Benge, 11c; Pivar, A156
73.80

**Small Bull** [1855–65]
*Petit taureau*

signed: BARYE incised, top side of base PL
 side
size: H. 3⅜″ (9.1cm); L. 5⅞″ (14.9cm); D. 2″
 (5.0cm)
patination: black over green
casting: sand; at least 3 pieces, including
 separate base
condition: tail repaired and patina altered;
 base abraded
lit.: Benge, 13; Pivar, A160
74.66

**\*Bull Brought Down by a Bear** 1830s (1839)
*Taureau terrassé par un ours*

signed: BARYE incised, PR side of base toward
 front
size: H. 5⅝″ (14.2cm); L. 11″ (28.0cm); D. 6″
 (15.2cm)
patination: black over green
casting: sand; 4 pieces
condition: irregular losses in patina
lit.: Benge, 111b; Pivar, A159
73.82

**\*Rearing Bull with Tiger** late 1830s (1837)
*Taureau cabré groupé avec un tigre*

signed: BARYE cast, top of base below bull's
 PR rear leg
size: H. 8½″ (21.7cm); L. 10¼″ (25.9cm);
 D. 4⅜″ (11.1cm)
patination: black over green
casting: sand; 11 pieces
condition: patina abraded on high points
lit.: Benge, 112; Pivar, A158
73.81

**Camel**

**Persian Camel** [1855–65]
*Petit Chameau de Perse*

signed: BARYE incised top of base, rear of
 center, PR side
size: H. 4½″ (11.6cm); L. 4¾″ (12.0cm);

 D. 1¾″ (4.4cm)
patination: green
casting: sand; probably 1 piece, including base
condition: patina damaged on legs, head, and
 base
lit.: Benge, 25 (as *Dromedary*); Pivar, A94
74.64

**Crocodile**

**\*Crocodile Devouring an Antelope** 1830s
*Crocodile dévorant une antilope*

signed: BARYE cast on top rear edge of base
size: H. 6⅜″ (16.2cm); L. 16⅜″ (41.6cm);
 D. 9″ (22.8cm)
patination: black over green
casting: sand; at least 3 pieces
condition: some losses in patination
lit.: Benge, 113d; Pivar, A195
73.85

**Deer**

**Axis** 1820s
*Axis*

signed: BARYE cast on side below PR leg; date
 below has been removed
size: H. 5⅛″ (12.9cm); L. 6⅝″ (16.8cm); D. 2″
 (5.0cm)
patination: green with black and brown
casting: sand; 6 pieces
condition: PR antler restored
lit.: Benge, 18d (as *Java Deer*); Pivar, A113
74.33

**Deer** (?) 1820s
*Axis*

signed: BARYE incised top of base, center PL
  side
size: H. 6½" (16.6cm); L. 6¾" (17.2cm);
  D. 1⅞" (4.9cm)
patination: black over green
casting: sand; 1 piece; some cold-working on
  hind quarters
condition: losses in patina; base abraded
lit.: Benge, 96 (as *Stag Walking*); Pivar, A116
  (as *Ganges Deer*)
74.35

**Doe Reclining** 1830s (1840)
*Biche couchée*

signed: BARYE cast and reinforced by incising
  on top front of base; date illegible
size: H. 3½" (9.0cm); L. 6" (15.4cm); D. 2½"
  (6.5cm)
patination: green with black highlights
casting: sand; 1 piece; same doe appears in
  73.76
condition: some abrasions in patina
lit.: Benge 22d; Pivar, A111
74.31

**Fawn Reclining** 1840
*Faon couché*

signed: BARYE cast and reinforced, top of
  base, PL front; 1840 cast, PL rear; also faint
  cast of personal stamp on top rear of base
size: H. 1⅞" (4.8cm); L. 6" (15.4cm); D. 2⅜"
  (6.0cm)
patination: dark green with overlying black
casting: sand; 1 piece
condition: losses in patina, especially on base
lit.: Benge, 32d; Pivar, A112
74.32

**Fawn Scratching** 1820s
*Faon se grattant*

signed: BARYE cast on base by tail
size: H. 2½" (6.5 cm); L. 6¼" (16.0cm);
  D. 3⅛" (8.0cm)
patination: reddish brown with traces of green
  and black
materials: fawn, brass; landscape base, bronze;
  marble base
casting: sand probably; 2 pieces, extensive
  cold-working; analyzed by the Scientific
  Research Lab, Winterthur Museum
lit.: Benge, 33; Pivar, A125
68.14

**Ganges Deer** (?) 1830s
*Cerf du Gange*

signed: BARYE cast on PL rear side of base;
  personal cold stamp BARYE faintly cast on
  PR rear of base; illegible images before and
  after stamp
size: H. 4⅞" (12.3cm); L. 6⅜" (16.3cm); D. 2"
  (5.1cm)
patination: green over reddish brown
casting: sand; 8 pieces; cold-working
condition: patina on base abraded
74.36

**Virginia Deer** (relief) (1831)
*Cerf de Virginie*

signed: Barye 4, stamp cast in lower PR corner
size: H. 5¾" (14.6cm); W. 8⅛" (20.5cm)
patination: blackish brown with thin bluish
  green
casting: sand; 1 piece and 2 hangers
condition: patina worn on antler; scratches in
  background
lit.: Pivar, R13
74.44

**Virginia Deer, Left Foot Raised** 1830s
*Cerf la jambe levée*

signed: BARYE incised on side, PL front
size: H. 6⅝" (16.9cm); L. 6¼" (16.0cm);
  D. 1⅞" (4.9cm)
patination: black over green
casting: sand; 9 pieces, including separate base
condition: both legs securing deer to base have
  been broken and repaired; PL antler bent
  inward; patina abraded on sides
lit.: Pivar, A115 (as *Axis Deer*)
73.78

**\*Virginia Deer Reclining** 1837
*Cerf de Virginie couché*

signed: BARYE 1837, cast and reinforced by
  incising, front of base PL side
size: H. 10" (25.3cm); L. 15⅞" (40.3cm);
  D. 7⅜" (18.8cm)
patination: green with thin upper layer of
  black
casting: sand; 3 pieces
condition: losses in patina on base and deer on
  the back, PL side
lit.: Benge, 19a; Pivar, A117
73.77
Fig. 16

**\*Elk Surprised by a Lynx** Salon of 1834
*Elan surpris par un lynx*

signed: BARYE cast and reinforced, PR front
  side of base; 3 illegible numbers to PL of
  signature
size: H. 9" (22.9cm); L. 13¼" (33.6cm); D. 6"
  (15.2)
patination: heavy, opaque black over green
casting: sand; 4 pieces, including separate base
condition: patina losses on upper back
lit.: Benge, 120b; Pivar, A99
73.74

***Stag, Doe, and Fawn** 1830s
*Cerf, biche, et faon*

signed: BARYE incised on top of base, PR center
size: H. 9⅛″ (23.1cm); L 9⅞″ (25.2cm); D. 5¾″ (14.5cm)
patination: black over green
casting: sand; at least 4 pieces, including separate base; deer in group appear individually and in other groupings
lit.: Benge, 99a: Pivar A110
73.76

***Ten-Point Stag Brought Down by Two Scotch Hounds** Salon of 1833
*Cerf dix cors terrassé par deux lévriers d'Ecosse*

signed: BARYE, PL upper top side of base, below dog's chest
size: H. 17″ (43.2cm); L. 22½″ (57.2cm); D. 12⅝″ (32.0cm)
patination: black over green
casting: sand; about 24 pieces, including separate base
lit.: Benge, 198b; Pivar, A104
73.75

## Eagle

***Eagle Holding a Heron** ca. 1845
*Aigle tenant un héron*

signed: BARYE incised on PR top of base
size: H. 12⅜″ (31.5cm); L. 12½″ (31.7cm); D. 9⅜″ (23.9cm)
patination: black over green
casting: sand; at least 6 pieces
condition: patina abraded on head and elsewhere; tips of wings bent
lit.: Benge, 117d; Pivar, A167
73.83

## Elephant

***African Elephant** 1830s
*Eléphant d'Afrique*

signed: BARYE cast, front PL top of base
size: H. 5⅛″ (13.1cm); L. 7⅞″ (20.1cm); D. 2⅝″ (6.8cm)
patination: heavy, opaque black over green
casting: sand; 3 pieces, including separate base
condition: many small losses in patina
lit.: Benge, 29i; Pivar, A89; Fogg, 23
73.68

## Genet

***Genet Carrying Off a Bird** (relief) (1831)
*Genette emportant un oiseau*

signed: BARYE incised lower center; 11 incised on reverse center, lower edge
size: H. 5⅜″ (13.8cm); W. 7⅝″ (19.3cm)
patination: brown with thin bluish-green highlights; brownish black on groundline and figures
casting: sand; 1 piece and 2 hangers
condition: patina worn on figures; top and

bottom edge damaged
lit.: Benge, 121; Pivar, R12
74.43

## Greyhound

***Tom, Algerian Greyhound** (reduction) [1855–65]
*Tom, lévrier d'Algérie*

signed: BARYE incised, side of base beneath PR rear leg
size: H. 7½″ (19.2cm); L. 14¼″ (36.2cm); D. 4⅜″ (11.0cm)
patination: black over green
casting: sand; 8 pieces, including separate base
condition: patina abraded on high points and base
lit.: Benge, 37; Pivar, A14
74.24
Fig. 20

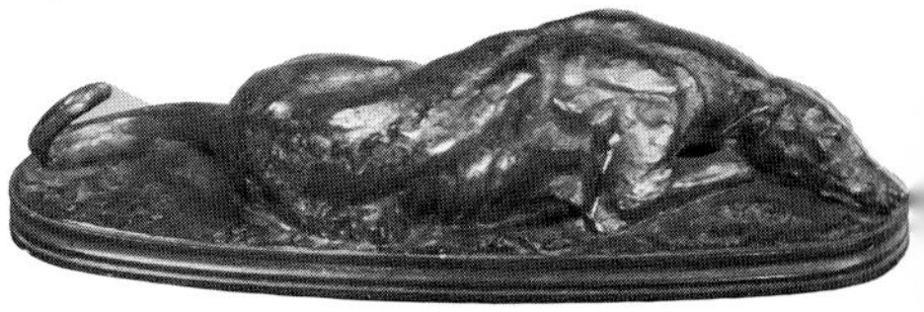

**Reclining Greyhound** 1830s
*Lévrier couché*
signed: BARYE cast on top of base, PR rear
size: H. 2½″ (6.3cm); L. 10⅜″ (26.3cm); D. 3½″ (8.9cm)
patination: thin black over bright green
casting: sand; 1 piece
condition: high points slightly abraded
lit.: Benge, 38b; Pivar, A13
74.27

***Greyhound Retrieving a Hare** [1855–65]
*Levrette rapportant un lièvre*

signed: BARYE incised, center PL side of base
size: H. 8¼″ (21.0cm); L. 13⅝″ (34.5cm); D. 3¾″ (9.5cm)
patination: thin black over dark green
casting: sand; 5 pieces, including separate base
condition: losses in patina on dog and rabbit
lit.: Benge, 122b; Pivar, A15
73.94

## Horse

**\*Half-Blood Horse, with Head Down** 1830s
*Cheval demi-sang la tête baissée*

signed: BARYE cast and reinforced by incising,
PR rear top of base
size: H. 7⅝″ (19.3cm); L. 11¾″ (30.0cm);
D. 3¾″ (9.7cm)
patination: transparent reddish brown with
traces of dark brown and green
casting: sand probably; 8 pieces
lit.: Benge, 42d; Pivar, A147
73.70
Fig. 15

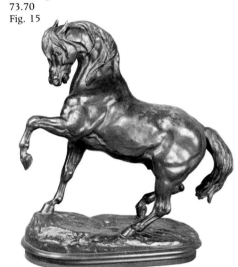

**Turkish Horse** (left foreleg raised) 1830s
*Cheval turc, autre*

signed: BARYE cast on top of base behind PR leg
size: H. 10½″ (26.7cm); L. 10″ (25.4cm);
D. 4¾″ (12.0cm)
patination: black over green; appearance is black
casting: sand; 2 pieces, including separate base
condition: several plugs to repair flaws on
neck of horse and in signature; patina
damaged on PR lower edge of base
lit.: Benge, 44h; Pivar, A150
73.72

**\*Turkish Horse** (right foreleg raised) 1830s
*Cheval turc*

signed: BARYE cast and probably reinforced
on PL top center of base
size: H. 10½″ (26.7cm); L. 10″ (25.4cm);
D. 4½″ (11.5cm)
patination: black over green; appearance is
dark green
casting: sand; approximately 2 pieces,
including separate base
lit.: Benge, 44g; Pivar, A149; Fogg, 20
73.71
Fig. 14

**\*Horse Attacked by a Lion** Salon of 1833
*Cheval surpris par un lion*

signed: BARYE incised on PR front side of base
size: H. 15¾″ (39.9cm); L. 15⅛ (38.3cm);
D. 5¼″ (13.3)
patination: black over green
casting: sand; approximately 14 pieces,
including separate base
lit.: Benge, 125d; Pivar, A146
73.69
Fig. 28

## Jaguar

**Sleeping Jaguar** 1830s
*Jaguar dormant*

signed: BARYE cast and reinforced by incising,
PL rear top of base
size: H. 3⅜″ (8.5cm); L. 12¼″ (31.2cm); D. 6″
(15.4cm)
patination: black over green
casting: sand; 1 piece
condition: surface disfigured by major losses in
patina
lit.: Benge, 46e; Pivar, A84
73.64

**Standing Jaguar** 1830s (1840)
*Jaguar debout*, No. 1

signed: BARYE incised on side of base below
PR front paw
size: H. 5⅛″ (13.1cm); L. 8⅞″ (22.5cm);
D. 2¾″ (7.0cm)
patination: dark green
casting: sand; 1 piece
condition: surface disfigured by losses in
patina
lit.: Benge 47c: Pivar, A78
73.63

**Walking Jaguar** 1830s
*Jaguar qui marche*

signed: BARYE cast, PR top front of base
size: H. 5″ (12.8cm); L. 9″ (23.0cm); D. 2⅞″
(7.4cm)
patination: heavy, opaque black over green
casting: sand; probably 2 pieces (jaguar and
base)
condition: minor scratches and abrasions
lit.: Benge, 48c; Pivar, A76
73.62

## Jaguar Devouring a Crocodile 1830s [1850P]
*Jaguar dévorant un crocodile*

signed: BARYE cast and reinforced by incising,
top of base PL side of jaguar
size: H. 3⅛″ (8.0cm); L. 9½″ (24.3cm); D. 3¾″
(9.6cm)
patination: black over bluish green
casting: sand; 3 pieces
lit.: Benge, 127d; Pivar, A85
73.65
Fig. 37

**\*Jaguar Devouring a Hare** Salon of 1850–51
*Jaguar tenant un lièvre*

signed: A.L. BARYE, PL center of base
size: H. 17″ (43.2cm); L. 40″ (101.6cm);
D. 16⅞″ (43.0cm)
patination: black over green
casting: sand; 13 pieces, including separate
base
condition: patina worn in high points and
restored
lit.: Benge, 128c; Pivar, A82
74.67
Figs. 6, 36

## Leopard

**Leopard** (relief) 1831
*Léopard*

signed: BARYE incised lower PL; incised 111
on reverse center, lower edge
size: H. 5⅜″ (13.8cm); W. 7⅝″ (19.3cm)
patination: green over black
casting: sand; 1 piece and 2 hangers
condition: patina worn on high points and
corners
lit.: Benge, 52a; Pivar, R10
74.41

## Lion

**\*Lion of the Column of July** (relief)
(reduction) ca. 1838
*Lion de la Colonne de Juillet*

signed: BARYE incised right front edge of base
size: H. 8″ (20.4cm); W. 16¾″ (42.5cm);
D. 2½″ (6.4cm)
patination: black over green
casting: sand; 1 piece
lit.: Benge, 62f; Pivar, R7; Fogg, 16
73.89
Fig. 13

**\*Seated Lion** (reduction) ca. 1836
*Lion assis*, No. 1

signed: BARYE cast and reinforced on top of
    base, PL rear corner
size: H. 14¼" (36.1cm); L. 12⅝" (32.2cm);
    D. 6¾" (17.0cm)
patination: black over green
casting: sand; 3 pieces, including separate base
lit.: Benge, 55l; Pivar, A42
73.49
Fig. 11

**\*Walking Lion** (1836)
*Lion qui marche*

signed: BARYE cast on top of base, PL front
    corner
size: H. 8⅞" (22.6cm); L. 16⅜" (41.5cm);
    D. 4⅛" (10.4cm)
patination: black over green
casting: sand; 2 pieces (lion and base)
condition: patina losses on rib cage, mane, and
    face
lit.: Benge, 59p; Pivar, A48
73.52

**Lioness of Algeria** 1830s
*Lionne d'Algérie*

signed: BARYE cast and reinforced by incising
    on center top of base under lioness
size: H. 8" (20.2cm); L. 10⅜" (26.3cm);
    D. 3⅜" (8.6cm)
patination: brownish black over green
casting: sand; 2 pieces (lioness and base)
condition: tail damaged; small losses of patina
    overall
lit.: Benge, 64e; Pivar, A47
73.51

**\*Lioness of Senegal** 1830s
*Lionne du Sénégal*

signed: BARYE cast on top center of base
    under body
size: H. 7⅞" (20.0cm); L. 11⅝" (29.5cm);
    D. 3⅜" (8.7cm)

patination: black with green underlayer and
    faint reddish-brown highlights
casting: sand; at least 2 pieces (lioness and
    base)
lit.: Benge, 64f; Pivar, A46
73.50

**Lion Devouring a Doe** 1837
*Lion dévorant une biche*

signed: BARYE 1837, cast on top of base, PR
    rear corner; BARYE personal stamp cast on
    top of base, center front
size: H. 5¼" (13.5 cm); L. 12¼" (31.2cm);
    D. 7½" (19.2cm)
patination: black over green
casting: sand; 2 pieces
condition: minor abrasions and losses in
    patina
lit.: Benge, 131f; Pivar, A36
73.47

**\*Lion Crushing a Serpent** (reduction)
    ca. 1832
*Lion au Serpent*

signed: BARYE cast and possibly reinforced,
    PL top rear corner
size: H. 9⅞" (25.0cm); L. 14⅛" (35.9cm);
    D. 7¼" (18.5cm)
patination: green over black
casting: sand probably; 6 pieces, including
    separate base
condition: patina losses, especially under lion's
    torso
lit.: Benge, 134f; Pivar, A37; Fogg, 14
73.48
Fig. 31

**\*Two Young Lions** 1830s
*Deux jeunnes lions*

signed: BARYE cast on top of base
size: H. 6⅞" (17.6cm); L. 6¾" (17.1cm); D. 6"
    (15.2cm)
patination: green highlights over reddish
    brown
casting: sand; at least 6 pieces; extensive cold-
    working; analyzed by the Scientific Research
    Lab, Winterthur Museum
lit.: Benge, 137; Pivar, A34
73.46

Ocelot
_____

**\*Ocelot Carrying Off a Heron** ca. 1845
*Ocelot emportant un héron*

signed: BARYE cast and probably reinforced
    by incising on top of base, PL rear, below
    tail
size: H. 6⅞" (17.4cm); L. 12⅜" (31.5cm);
    D. 6½" (16.6cm)
patination: black over green
casting: sand; 12 pieces
condition: pinpoint losses of patina; high
    points abraded and retouched
lit.: Benge, 139h; Pivar, A86; Fogg, V
73.66

Panther
_____

**Panther** (relief) 1831
*Panthère*

signed: BARYE incised lower PL of design field
size: H. 5⅜" (13.8cm); W. 7½" (19.2cm)
patination: green over black
casting: sand; 1 piece and 2 hangers

condition: high points and edges abraded
lit.: Benge, 71g; Pivar, R11
74.42

**Reclining Panther** 1830s
*Panthère couchée*

signed: BARYE cast and reinforced by incising
  on top of base, PR front corner
size: H. 2½″ (6.5cm); L. 7⅜″ (18.6cm); D. 2¾″
  (7.0cm)
patination: thin black over green
casting: sand; 1 piece
condition: losses in patina on head, neck, and
  shoulders
lit.: Benge, 68f (as *Panther of India*); Pivar,
  A71; Fogg, IV (as *Panther of Tunis*)
74.28

**\*Panther of India** 1830s [1840P]
*Panthère de l'Inde*

signed: BARYE cast on PL side of base
size: H. 4⅞″ (12.4cm); L. 10⅝″ (27.1cm);
  D. 3¾″ (9.4cm)
patination: heavy, opaque black over green
casting: sand; 1 piece
condition: abraded patina, especially on edge
  of base
lit.: Benge, 67; Pivar, A72; Fogg, 21
  (as *Reclining Panther*)
73.59

**Panther of Tunis** 1830s (1840)
*Panthère de Tunis*

signed: BARYE cast on PL side of base
size: H. 5⅜″ (13.6cm); L. 10¾″ (27.5cm);
  D. 3⅞″ (9.7cm)
patination: heavy, opaque black over green
casting: sand; 1piece
condition: scratches and abrasion in patina,
  especially on edge of base
lit.: Benge, 69; Pivar, A73
73.60

**\*Panther Seizing a Stag** 1830s
*Panthère saisissant un cerf*

signed: A.L. BARYE cast on PL side top of
  base; BARYE reinforced by incising
size: H. 14″ (35.5cm); L. 22″ (56.0cm);
  D. 10¼″ (26.0cm)
patination: black over green
casting: sand; approximately 16 pieces,
  including separate base
lit.: Benge, 145e; Pivar, A70
73.58

**\*Panther Surprising a Civet Cat** 1830s
*Panthère surprenant un zibeth*

signed: BARYE cast on PR front side of base
size: H. 4¼″ (10.9cm); L. 9⅜″ (23.9cm);
  D. 3⅜″ (8.7cm)
patination: transparent black over green
casting: sand; at least 2 pieces
condition: gouges on base
lit.: Benge, 142e; Pivar, A74
73.61

**Parakeet**

**\*Parakeet Seated on a Tree** 1820s
*Perruche posée sur un arbre*

signed: BARYE incised on base at rear of tree
size: H. 7⅞″ (20.0cm); L. 5⅜″ (13.8cm);
  D. 4″ (10.2cm)

patination: green over black
casting: sand; at least 5 pieces
condition: patina worn in high points of base
  and tree
lit.: Benge, 73; Pivar, A172 (as *Parrot in a
  Tree*)
74.37

**Pheasant**

**\*Pheasant** (head to left) 1840s
*Faisan*

signed: BARYE cast on PL rear of base
size: H. 4¾″ (12.0cm); L. 8¼″ (20.9cm);
  D. 2⅜″ (6.0cm)
patination: green over reddish brown
casting: sand; at least 2 pieces (pheasant and
  base)
condition: patina damaged around claws
lit.: Benge, 74e; Pivar, A174
74.38

**Pheasant** (head to right) 1840s
*Faisan*

signed: BARYE cast and reinforced on front PR
  edge of base
size: H. 4¼″ (10.9cm); L. 8¼″ (20.9cm);
  D. 2⅜″ (6.0cm)
patination: dark green over thin reddish
  brown
casting: sand; probably 3 pieces, including
  separate base
condition: casting crack under PR side of tail;
  tail bent; losses in patina on high points,
  damaged tail, and around claws
lit.: Benge, 74f
74.39

**Pointer**

**Pointer** 1830s?
*Braque*

signed: BARYE cast on top of base, PR rear
  corner
size: H. 3¾″ (9.4cm); L. 7⅛″ (18.1cm); D. 2⅜″
  (6.0cm)
patination: transparent greenish brown with
  overlying black in recesses

materials: high zinc content
casting: sand; 2 pieces (dog and base); extensive cold-working; analyzed by the Scientific Research Lab, Winterthur Museum
lit.: Pivar, A19
68.15

### Python

***Python Crushing a Crocodile** ca. 1835–40 (1840)
*Python étouffant un crocodile*

signed: A.L. BARYE cast and reinforced by incising on top of base, PR corner
size: H. $6\frac{3}{8}$" (16.1cm); L. $15\frac{1}{4}$" (38.7cm); D. $5\frac{3}{4}$" (14.5cm)
patination: black over brown
casting: sand; at least 7 pieces, including separate base
lit.: Benge, 146; Pivar, A198
73.88
Fig. 35

***Python Crushing a Gazelle** 1830s
*Python enlacant une gazelle*

signed: A.L. BARYE cast on front PR side of base; BARYE reinforced
size: H. 6" (15.3cm); L. $15\frac{3}{8}$" (39.0cm); D. $5\frac{3}{4}$" (14.6cm)
patination: black over green
casting: sand; 9 pieces; analyzed by the Scientific Research Lab, Winterthur Museum
condition: finishing rough; joins visible; sections misaligned
lit.: Benge, 148c; Pivar, A197
73.87
Fig. 34

### Rabbit

**Rabbits** 1820s
*Lapins sur terrasse carrée*

signed: BARYE incised, top of PR front base
size: H. $2\frac{1}{4}$" (5.8cm); L. $3\frac{5}{8}$" (9.2cm); D. 2" (5.0cm)
patination: turquoise green with traces of overlying black
casting: sand; 3 pieces (2 rabbits and base)
condition: patina damaged on base
lit.: Benge, 78; Pivar, A187-8
74.30

### Ratel

***Ratel Stealing Eggs** [1855–65]
*Ratel dénichant des oeufs*

signed: BARYE incised on PL rear edge of base
size: H. $4\frac{3}{8}$" (11.1cm); L. $6\frac{3}{8}$" (16.2cm); D. $3\frac{1}{8}$" (8.0cm)
patination: black over green
casting: sand; 2 pieces; minor cold-working
lit.: Benge, 149; Pivar, A162
74.58

### Tiger

***Walking Tiger** 1830s (1836)
*Tigre qui marche*

signed: BARYE cast on top of base, in front of PR rear paw
size: H. $8\frac{1}{4}$" (20.9cm); L. 17" (43.2cm); D. 4" (10.3cm)
patination: brownish black over green
casting: sand; 3 pieces, including separate base
lit.: Benge, 104p; Pivar, A58; Fogg, 18
73.53

***Tiger Attacking an Antelope** ca. 1834?
*Tigre surprenant une antilope*

signed: BARYE cast on PR side of base
size: H. 13" (33.0cm); L. $21\frac{1}{4}$" (54.0cm); D. $10\frac{1}{4}$" (26.0cm)
patination: black over green
casting: sand; at least 5 pieces, including separate base
lit.: Benge, 156d; Pivar, A59
73.54
Fig. 30

**Tiger Attacking a Stag** Salon of 1830
*Tigre surprenant un cerf*

signed: BARYE cast top of base, center rear
size: H. $6\frac{1}{4}$" (15.9cm); L. $12\frac{1}{4}$" (31.2cm); D. 6" (15.3cm)
patination: red brown with overlying green and black
casting: sand; 8 pieces
lit.: Benge, 165; Pivar, A60
73.55
Fig. 29

***Tiger Devouring a Gavial** (reduction) ca. 1831
*Tigre dévorant un gavial*

signed: BARYE incised on top of base, center front
size: H. $7\frac{5}{8}$" (19.3cm); L. 20" (50.9cm); D. $7\frac{1}{2}$" (19.0cm)
patination: black over green
casting: sand; 3 pieces
condition: gavial's tail bent; patina abraded on high points, gavial's head, extended leg, and base
lit.: Benge, 160c; Pivar, A61
73.56
Fig. 27

**Tiger Devouring a Gazelle** 1834P
*Tigre dévorant une gazelle*

signed: BARYE cast and reinforced by incising on top front base, PR side
size: H. $5\frac{3}{8}$" (13.6cm); L. $13\frac{5}{8}$" (34.6cm); D. $5\frac{5}{8}$" (14.3cm)
patination: black over green
casting: sand; 4 pieces
lit.: Benge, 153f; Pivar, A62
73.57

### Turtle

**Turtle** 1820s
*Tortue*

signed: BARYE stamped center underside
size: H. $1\frac{1}{8}$" (2.9cm); L. $3\frac{5}{8}$" (9.2cm); D. $2\frac{3}{4}$" (7.0cm)
patination: transparent brown with overlying black and green
casting: sand?; 2 pieces
lit.: Benge, 105; Pivar, A192
Gift of Robert Wiles
1976.9

### Wolf

***Walking Wolf** [1855–65]
*Loup marchant*

signed: BARYE cast on middle PR side of base
size: H. $9\frac{1}{2}$" (24.2cm); L. $15\frac{1}{4}$" (38.9cm); D. $4\frac{1}{8}$" (10.5cm)
patination: black over green
casting: sand; 3 pieces, including separate base
lit.: Benge, 108c; Pivar, A32; Fogg, 26
73.95

**\*Wolf Seizing a Stag by the Throat** 1830s
*Loup tenant un cerf à la gorge*

signed: BARYE cast on base, PL rear corner

size: H. 8½" (21.5cm); L. 18⅞" (48.0cm);
  D. 5½ (14.0cm)
patination: heavy, opaque black over green
casting: sand; at least 11 pieces
lit.: Benge, 151b; Pivar, A31
73.45

**Two Light Candelstick** before 1847
*Flambeau bout de table à deux lumières*

signed: BARYE incised on edge of base
size: H. 9⅞" (25.1cm); L. 10½" (26.6cm);
  Diam. 3⅜" (8.6cm)
patination: green over black
casting: sand probably; 8 pieces, not including
  2 detached sleeves; underside of base has
  been spun
lit.: Benge, 242; Pivar D16
74.54

## Decorative Arts

**\*Candelstick with Leaves and Clochettes
  with a Scarab on the Stem** before 1847
*Flambeau décoré de feuillage et de clochettes, avec
  scarabée à la tige*

signed: BARYE incised under ivy/grape leaf on
  base
size: H. 12⅝" (32.0cm); D. 5¼" (13.5cm)
patination: black over green
casting: sand probably; at least 6 pieces
condition: leg of beetle slightly bent; candle
  cup may not be original
lit.: Benge, 234; Pivar, D15
74.57

**\*Candelstick, Greek Style with Antique
  Medallions** 1847-55
*Flambeau Grec avec médaillons antiques*

signed: BARYE incised on bottom of base
size: H. 10⅜" (26.5cm); D. 4⅝" (11.7cm)
patination: green over black; appearance is
  dark
casting: sand probably; possibly 11 pieces,
  including base; interior of cup and underside
  of base have been spun; some sections
  threaded, others joined
lit.: Benge, 238; Pivar, D14
74.52
Fig. 70

**\*Candelstick, Cup Form, with Arabesques,
  Bell Flowers, Owls, and Panthers' Heads**
  before 1847
*Flambeau*

signed: BARYE incised on edge of base
size: H. 6⅞" (17.5cm); D. 3⅜" (8.6cm)
patination: green
casting: sand; at least 7 pieces
lit.: Benge, 236
74.55
Fig. 68

**Candelstick with Volubilis, Roots, and
  Fawn's Feet with a Serpent about the
  Stem** before 1847
*Flambeau orné de volubilis, racines, et pieds de
  faune avec serpent à la tige*

signed: BARYE incised PR side of foot below
  snake's head
size: H. 9½" (24.2cm); L. 3⅝" (9.1cm); D. 3¼"
  (8.4cm)
patination: green over black
casting: sand; at least 6 pieces; foot matches 74.45
condition: feet and knees abraded
lit.: Benge, 237; Pivar, D12
74.51

**\*Three Light Candelabra Antique Style with
  Chains** ca. 1845
*Candélabra antique à trois lumières, decoré
  d'arabesques et de chaines, surmonté d'une
  cigogne*

signed: BARYE incised, underside of one leg
size: H. 26¼" (66.5cm); D. 8½" (21.6cm)
patination: black over green
casting: sand?; at least 25 pieces per
  candlestick, plus rings and chains
condition: damaged patina; chains and rings
  on one are possible replacement; stork
  finials missing
lit.: Benge, 231c; Pivar, D6
74.48
Fig. 66

**\*Card Receiver with Fawn's Feet, Grapes**
  before 1847
*Coupe pieds de faunes et raisins*

signed: BARYE cold stamped on outside edge
  of base
size: H. 4⅛" (10.4cm); Diam. 7⅝" (19.4cm);
  Diam. of base 3⅜" (8.5cm)
patination: shiny dark brown over black
casting: sand; 3 pieces, including base; cold-
  working; edges of plate spun; foot matches
  74.51; several elements identical with 74.46
condition: inactive corrosion on top of plate;
  one leaf on base damaged
lit.: Benge, 243
74.45

**\*Nine Light Candelabra with Six Figures,
Masks, and Chimeras** ca. 1840 (1846)
*Candélabra à neuf lumières, decoré de six figures,
mascarons, et chimères*

signed: BARYE cast, top of base beneath
   peacock
size: H. 26″ (66.2cm); Diam. of arms 16½″
   (41.9cm); Diam. of base 8″ (20.3cm)
patination: black over green
casting: sand; more than 40 pieces each
condition: damaged patina; arms loose and
   repaired; finial of Three Graces missing
lit.: Benge, 230e; Pivar, D9
74.49
Fig. 65

**\*Card Receiver with Inverted Border on
High Stem** before 1847
*Coupe à bords reversés, haute tige*

signed: BARYE incised top edge of base
size: H. 5⅞″ (14.9cm); Diam. 7¼″ (18.4cm);
   Diam. of base 3⅜″ (8.6cm)
patination: green over black, matte and rough,
   moire pattern underside of plate
casting: probably sand; 5 pieces, including
   base; cold-working; several elements
   identical to 74.45
lit.: Benge, 244
74.46
Fig. 69

---

# Watercolors

---

**\*Two Lions Resting** 1830s?
*Deux lions au repos*

signed: right, BARYE
size: H. 11½″(29.2cm); W. 18½″ (47.0cm)
lit.: Zieseniss, A 43
76.18
Fig. 72

**\*Tiger Hunt** late 1830s?
*Chasse au tigre*

signed: left, BARYE
watercolor over charcoal
size: H. 20⅛″ (51.0cm); W. 27½″ (70.0cm)
lit.: Zieseniss, E 10
76.19
Fig. 74

**\*Tiger Searching for a Track** 1830s?
*Tigre cherchant une piste*

signed: right, BARYE
size: H. 6½″ (16.5cm); W. 9¾″ (24.7cm)
lit.: Zieseniss, B 41
Bequest of William A. Clark
26.5
Fig. 73